The
'Old Cornwall'
CHRISTMAS
ANTHOLOGY

Dedication

To Sandra and Bryn,
who have lived with this for so long.

The 'Old Cornwall'
CHRISTMAS
ANTHOLOGY

Compiled by

George Pritchard

Federation of Old Cornwall Societies

Published by the
Federation of Old Cornwall Societies
Wingfield, 5, British Road,
St Agnes, Cornwall
TR5 0TX

www.oldcornwall.org

ISBN 978 0902660 43 4

Printed and bound in Cornwall by R Booth Ltd
The Praze, Penryn, TR10 9AA

CONTENTS

Foreword   6

Introduction   7

Acknowledgements   8

Christmas Traditions   9
*Superstitions – Customs – Date of New Year's Day – Bygone
Christmases - The Christmas Block - Nick-a-Nan-Night –
Guise Dancing – The Cornish Christmas Bush*

Food & Drink   44
*Christmas Food - That Real Ambrosia - Pies - Other dishes -
Christmas Drinks - The Christmas and the Dilly – Cornish Saffron
Cake - Chirky Wheeler – Market Reports – Feeding the Poor at
Christmas – Christmas Eve at Jamaica Inn*

Cornish Carols   80
*The Carol Singers [poem] – Stratton Carol of the Months –
The Dilly Song – Dilly Carol [Gwennap Version] –Padstow
Carol Singing – Thomas Merritt*

Christmas News   103
From various sources

Christmas Games   113
Card Games - Party Games

The Cornish Play   124
*[Christmas Play] by Uncle Jan Trenoodle - A Redruth
Christmas Play - A Guise Dance Play, St Keverne*

The Wassail   133

Christmas Ghost Stories   140
The Piskies in the Cellar - The Ghost of Rosewarne - Betty Toddy

Poems for Christmas   150
*For the Postwoman at Christmas – A Christmas Carol composed by
Atty White... – The White Ladie – Dolly Pentreath's Christmas - How
the Parson Caught his Fish on Christmas Day*

Cornish Christmas Abroad   164

Foreword

Christmastide is very special, and its religious significance has influenced the people of Cornwall like those further afield, but the ways in which it has been celebrated here over the centuries have not all been replicated elsewhere. There will be nostalgic echoes of festivals at home for almost anyone who reads this book, but there will also be the differences which make Cornwall Cornish.

'Old Cornwall' Societies have the motto, "Cuntelleugh an brewyon us gesys na vo kellys travyth", or "Gather the fragments that remain..." and have followed this guidance for over 90 years. From the collected records of our local traditions and culture which have found their way into the pages of the 'Old Cornwall' journal and the archives of individual Societies, George Pritchard, has sifted and sorted a fascinating variety of those relating to Cornish Christmases. To them he has added extensively from Victorian books, local newspapers, other journals and the internet - obviously a labour of love.

So, we can revel in the enduring glow of Christmases past with carols and carolling, ambitious meals and the varied seasonal recipes of yesteryear, the Christmas fun and games, the customs of former times, the guise-dancing, the dutiful munificence of the gentry to those less fortunate, and charity at the workhouse; and we can enjoy humour in dialect yarns, poems, ghost stories, and much more.

Terry Knight
President, Federation of 'Old Cornwall' Societies, 2009-12.

Introduction

Nowadays, each year, preparations for Christmas seem to start earlier. On every hand the commerce involved in merry-making and the promotion of means of enjoyment hold out strong temptations. It needs only the inclination and a full purse for commercial enterprise to be well rewarded. The internet advertises books on decorative arts and crafts, crackers, gifts and gadgets—endless in variety and at prices to suit all pockets. The butcher will take orders for the best turkey, goose, duck, pork or joint of beef which the Cornish so greatly value. In supermarket and grocery shop, mountains of dates and pyramids of Christmas-puddings almost block the aisles. As to the confectioners, they were enticing enough to us in our childhood, but they are positively maddening now. Such attractions as the beautiful boxes containing chocolates, and sweets, and the radiant bon-bons, all in their many-hued tinsel garbs entice us through the door. The silver-berried mistletoe, the thousand-and-one ornaments and eatables for the Christmas tree, to be admired by adults and children, lure all who have enjoyments in store to the ever-welcome season.

In past times in Cornwall people still held to traditional beliefs that on Christmas night the bees would sing in their hives for gladness, and at midnight the cattle in the fields would kneel down in mute adoration. In royal palace, lordly mansion, or the humblest cottage, even in the cold workhouse and the dismal gaol, there was either rejoicing or anticipation of the morrow. With the internet undreamt of, local newspapers advertised books on decorative work; and mottos, wreaths, devices—endless in variety and at prices to suit all pockets. The butcher intimated that the primest beast he had ever handled would be sacrificed at the shrine of that roast beef which the Cornish so much esteem. In the grocer's shop mountains of figs, pyramids of currants, luscious candied fruits, neatly-arranged almonds and raisins, would appeal to those who could afford a plum-pudding. The children dreamt of the taste of oranges and nuts, and of bells, tapers, flags and lanterns on the Christmas tree, hoping good St. Nicholas would glide to their bedsides and leave presents and *his* benediction. The bright berries and prickly leaves of the holly glistened in parlour and kitchen; the yule log and ashen faggot blazed; and "wassail, wassail" echoed in hall and drawing-room. The streets and farmyards resounded with carols, some centuries old in words and tunes, which Mr. Davies Gilbert had collected and preserved; joined by others more modern, written by the local organists and even by miners on their way to core.

I hope that I have relayed all of these things in this book and that you enjoy reading of Christmas Past in Cornwall.

George Pritchard
Penhalvean, Cornwall.

Acknowledgements

My thanks to the staff of the Cornwall Centre, Redruth, the Morrab Library, Penzance, and to the members of Old Cornwall Societies who collected the fragments. Also to Mary Vingoe who told her grandson William Bottrell ('Old Celt') the family stories and inspired him to become the foremost 19th century recorder of Cornish Folklore.

Special thanks to Anne Knight for her patience and encouragement whilst proof reading and to Terry Knight for his help with the layout.

CHRISTMAS TRADITIONS
Superstitions

Margaret A. Courtney. *Cornish Feasts and Folklore*, 1890.

Quoting "a friend", the author says:

I suppose the time to which I refer is over forty years ago. After making up a large turf fire, for hot 'umers' (embers) and pure water are absolutely necessary in these divinations, the young people left the house in single file, to pull the rushes and gather the ivy-leaves by means of which they were to learn whether they were to be married, and to whom; and if any, or how many, of their friends were to die before the end of the year. On leaving and on returning each of these twelfth-night diviners touched the 'cravel' with the forehead and 'wished'. The cravel is the tree that preceded lintels in chimney corners, and its name from this custom may have been derived from 'to crave'. Had any of the party inadvertently broken the silence before the rushes and ivy-leaves had been procured they would all have been obliged to retrace their steps to the house and again touch the cravel; but this time all went well.

 When we came back, those who wished to know their fate named the rushes in pairs, and placed them in the hot embers; one or two of the engaged couples being too shy to do this for themselves, their friends, amidst much laughing, did it for them. The manner in which the rushes burned showed if the young people were to be married to the person chosen or not; some of course burnt well, others parted, and one or two went out altogether. The couples that burnt smoothly were to be wedded, and the one named after the rush that lasted longest outlived the other. This settled, one ivy-leaf was thrown on the fire; the number of cracks it made was the number of years before the wedding would take place. Then two were placed on the hot ashes; the cracks they gave this time showed how many children the two would have. We then drew ivy-leaves named after present or absent friends through a wedding-ring, and put them into a basin of water which we left until the next morning. Those persons whose leaves had shriveled or turned black in the night were to die before the next Twelfth-tide, and those who were so unfortunate as to find their leaves spotted with red, by some violent death, unless a 'pellar' (wise man) could by his skill and incantations

grant protection. These prophecies through superstition sometimes unluckily fulfilled themselves.

 Thomas Quiller Couch in the *Western Antiquary*, September, 1883.

Parties are general in Cornwall on New Year's-eve to watch in the New Year and wish friends health and happiness; but I know of no peculiar customs, except that before retiring to rest the old women opened their Bibles at haphazard to find out their luck for the coming year. The text upon which the forefinger of the right hand rested was supposed to foretell the future. And money, generally a piece of silver, was placed on the threshold, to be brought in the first thing on the following day, that there might be no lack of it for the year. Nothing was ever lent on New Year's-day, as little as possible taken out, but all that could be brought into the house. "I have even known the dust of the floor swept inwards."

 William Bottrell. *Traditions and Hearthside Stories of West Cornwall*, 2nd series, 1873.

There is a curious Christmas superstition connected with the Fogo, Vog, or Vow (local names for a cove) at Pendeen, in North St. Just. "At dawn on Christmas-day the spirit of the 'Vow'[1] has frequently been seen just within the entrance near the cove, in the form of a beautiful lady dressed in white, with a red rose in her mouth. There were persons living a few years since who had seen the fair but

---

1. See the White Ladie poem by Margaret Courtney.

not less fearful vision; for disaster was sure to visit those who intruded on the spirit's morning airing."

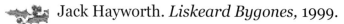 Jack Hayworth. *Liskeard Bygones,* 1999.

For centuries Cornish people have held that the Christmas Festivities should continue until the eve of Old Christmas Day, (6th January), after which all decorations are taken down. This date is also known as "Twelfth Night" and the custom is said to have been observed since the reign of Alfred. In those days a law was made with relation to holidays by which the twelve days after the nativity of our saviour were made festivals. During the reigns of Elizabeth 1st and James 1st the celebration of Twelfth Day was equal with Christmas Day, a festival throughout the land, and observed with pomp and ceremony in Universities, at Court, at the Temple and Lincoln's and Grey's Inns.

In a document dated 1562 appear the hospitable rites of St Stephen's Day, St John's Day and Twelfth day. They were ordered to be exactly alike and observed as such.

In the old days when superstitions were taken note of, one was on Twelfth Day, cattle should be fed a double ration of fodder and on failure to do so, the farmer would be overtaken with bad luck.

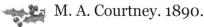 M. A. Courtney. 1890.

Door-steps on New Year's-day were formerly sanded for good luck, because I suppose people coming into the house were sure to bring some of it in with them sticking to their feet.

Customs

Britton and Brayley. *Devon and Cornwall illustrated*, 1831.

On St. Stephen's-day, 26th December, before the days of gun-licences, every man or boy who could by any means get a gun went out shooting, and it was dangerous to walk the lanes. The custom is said to have had its origin in the legend of one of St. Stephen's guards being awakened by a bird just as his prisoner was going to escape. A similar practice prevailed in the neighbourhood of Penzance on "Feasten Monday", the day after Advent Sunday; but on that day I have never heard of any religious idea connected with it.

In the week after Christmas-day a fair is held at Launceston (and also at Okehampton in Devonshire), called "giglet fair" (a "giglet or giglot" is a giddy young woman). It is principally attended by young people. "At this 'giglet market', or wife-market, the rustic swain was privileged with self-introduction to any of the nymphs around him, so that he had a good opportunity of choosing a suitable partner if tired of a single life."

There is one saint whose name is familiar to all in Cornwall, but whose sex is unknown. This saint has much to answer for; promises made, but never intended to be kept, are all to be fulfilled on next St. Tibb's-eve, a day that some folks say "falls between the old

13

and the new year"; others describe it as one that comes "neither before nor after Christmas."

Royal Cornwall Gazette, 3rd January 1835.

Paul: On Christmas Eve, the fishermen of Mousehole and Newlyn, lit up fifteen large candles on the pinnacles of Paul Tower, and there being no wind up they burnt as readily as if they had been in a room. These are very singular occurrences for the time of the year; but since the 26th the weather has changed and it has blown a gale from S to S.S.W. with very thick weather.

East Cornwall Times, 17th December 1859.

The inhabitants of Launceston and the public generally are respectfully informed that we the undersigned grocers of Launceston approving of the agreements of the tradesmen of the neighbouring towns do hereby unanimously agree to abolish the practise of giving what is usually called "Christmasing" the custom being very unsatisfactory.

Signed: Doidge & Nicholls, Jos. Splittigue, J. T. Planse, J. Powell.

Richard Edmonds. *Land's End District,* 1862.

On Christmas-eve, in East as well as West Cornwall, poor women, sometimes as many as twenty in a party, call on their richer neighbours asking alms. This is "going a gooding".

M. A. Courtney. 1890.

In a few remote districts on Christmas-eve children may be, after nightfall, occasionally (but rarely) found dancing around painted lighted candles placed in a box of sand. This custom was very general fifty years ago. The church towers, too, are sometimes illuminated. This of course, on

14

the coast can only be done in very calm weather. The tower of Zennor church (Zennor is a village on the north coast of Cornwall, between St. Ives and St. Just) was lit up in 1883, for the first time since 1866.

M. A. Courtney. 1890.

At Falmouth, the lower classes formerly expected from all the shopkeepers, of whom they bought any of their Christmas groceries, a slice of cake and a small glass of gin. Some of the oldest established trades-people still observe this custom; but it will soon be a thing of the past.

M. A. Courtney. 1890.

Many elderly people at the beginning of the present century still kept to the "old style", and held their Christmas-day on Epiphany. On the eve of that day they said "the cattle in the fields and stalls never lay down, but at midnight turned their faces to the east and fell on their knees." Twelfth-day (old Christmas-day) was a time of general feasting and merriment. Into the Twelfth-day cake were put a wedding-ring, a sixpence and a thimble. It was cut into as many portions as there were guests; the person who found the wedding-ring in his (or her) portion would be married before the year was out; the holder of the thimble would never be married, and the one that got the sixpence would die rich.

Danny Green, Redruth, 2011.

When a young boy in the 1940s I lived with the Harris family at Treloskan farm in Cury. A family tradition on Christmas morning was to take one of the Christmas puddings that were hanging from the beams in the dairy.

15

This was then sliced and served cold with sugar and clotted cream as part of the Breakfast.

The Date of New Year's Day

 *Royal Cornwall Gazette*, 21st December 1893.

Till 1751 the legal New Year's Day was on March 25th. With the exception of Sweden, Russia, and Greece — the two latter still cling to the "old" style — England was the last European nation to adopt the "new" or "Gregorian" style of commencing the year on January 1st. from the seventh to the thirteenth century the year in England was reckoned from Christmas.

Bygone Christmases

A New Year's Wish in Cornish, by R.M.N. *Old Cornwall,* Vol.1, No.4, 1924.

In a letter in English, written by John Boson to William Gwavas, and dated Newlyn, Dec. 25, 1709, he ends —"wishing you a *Loan blethan noueth, ha bennen joungk —ha mona lour gans goz Gureg*" - A Happy New Year, and a young woman, and plenty of money with your wife - *Bledhen Noweth Lowen, ha benen youank—ha mona lour gans agas gwreg* (Gwavas MSS. f.2).

West Briton, 3rd January 1840.

Bude: On Monday evening last, being old Christmas day, a subscription tea party, having for its object the promotion of temperance and sociability, was held in a suite of rooms in that commodious and well-known family house, once the favoured summer retreat of the Baronial family of Molesworth, the villa of Bude, built by the late Sir

John Arscot. The party, which consisted of nearly one hundred of the respectable inhabitants of Bude and its vicinity, began to assemble about five o'clock, and soon after six were served with tea and coffee in the large drawing-room fronting the sea, and the other rooms immediately adjoining.

An ample provision of the usual accompaniments to this elegant repast had been made under the direction of Miss Browne, assisted by several ladies of the place, whose individual and united exertions to please were crowned with complete success, as the whole party appeared not only highly gratified, but it may truly be said that cheerfulness and the best feelings pervaded the whole assembly.

Refreshments, consisting of twelfth-day cake, fruit, &c, were handed round in great abundance at intervals, during the evening; and a small band of excellent musicians were in attendance, and played a variety of pieces from the most eminent composers, in a style to draw forth the most rapturous applause of the assembled party. The hour of ten, the signal to break up, arrived much too soon for the company, who appeared to be in the full enjoyment of this first attempt at anything like a public coalescence of all sects and parties to spend an evening together in this pleasing and social way; and most, if not all of those present, have expressed their express desire to repeat it, at least annually, if not oftener. On the following evening, several of the aged poor of the place were regaled with what remained of the previous evening's entertainment.

West Briton, 27th December 1850.

Opening of an organ in the Wesleyan Chapel, St Ives: On the 10th instant, the Rev. R. YOUNG preached a sermon on the occasion of opening an organ in this chapel. And on Christmas-day, the Rev. E.R. TALBOT, and the Rev. W.P. BURGESS, of St. Ives, preached in connexion with the same. This instrument, which is introduced without any cost to the trustees has been erected by Messrs. Thomas HARVEY and William HARRY, who are both self-instructed. The organ will be paid for by subscription; it is pronounced an excellent instrument, and is a very great ornament to the chapel.

An Old Cornish Chres'muss (Cornish Dialect), by W. Arthur Pascoe. *Old Cornwall*, Vol.1, No.9, 1929.

Chres'muss ednt like a use to be, fifty er sexty 'ear agone. Caugh, darn'ee, I kin mind the time when Chres'muss wus more like Chres'muss, es you mit say! Sexty 'ear agone, ded I tell'ee ? . . . Nigher sebenty, I reckon; cus come nex' Mikklemuss en a vortnit, I shull be four score an' dree, so I s'pose I'm what they call an autogenarium, railly, ace, a brave age, edna you? I've a renned a purty good coose, I'll warn'ee. But, caugh, simmin to me e dawnt sim nawthen to look back 'pon.

Why I was telling me li'l grandcheeld awnly a mite agone, wot capers there wus when I wus a boy. When I says "boy," I mean o' coose when I wus a brave upstanden chap. Left skule then, ded'ee say? No, I never had a mort o' what you mit call- skulin, Mester. I larned all I knave, I b'leve, mezell. Not that th' oxen out t' field, an' thickey ol 'oss I

18

used to harvey wi', dedn't larn me a bravish passel, wan way or t'other. Ace, ace, passhens, parseverans, and obadience to they as desarve it, they cattle larned me.

But, yer, study now! Sims, Mester, as though I'm like Bodmint shoemakers on 'ossback, "allus want to gallop uphill." Twus Chres'muss we wus on 'pon, wadn't a? Lor' bless me days, I'd a clane fergot! Scat my rags, what a proper time we used to hev, to be sure!

Talk about a spray; never see nawthen like they days again! They'm gone, Mester, an' mores the pity, I say. Curls and darkey-parties; wassail drinkin'; goodin's; rum an' baccy, brot in by night from the coasts; cider an' caake, so much es you c'd ait, in the farmers kitchens, an' the yellow "neck," hanged up to the highest beam, glisterin' like gold agen the blazin' Chres'muss mock.—Dear, dear, tes whisht to think they days es past an' gone! Niver mind, we'm better off in some respec's, to be sure.

Like to knaw, would'ee, summin about et? Now, I'll tell'ee, so well's I kin, what Chres'muss Aive wus like, dree score an ten 'ears back.

Darn'ee, Mester, you ought to ha seed tha doin's awver Lesquithick when I wus a mite of a tackar there in farm sarvice—net very big fer me age, but brave'n' sharp an forthy-like, I rec'lect. Missus (that wud be th' ol Mis' Tervenen in they days) her says to me, her saith, "Wi'yum, boy, what about the firing fer Chres'muss Aive? I've a 'slocked Mester 'Venen," her saith, "to fetch home the Chres'muss mock 'pon the dray, but I shall want a few ashen vaggits besides, to burn wi' mun an' make the fire fitty."

"Daunt you git in no pore about that, Missus," I saith; "I'll see you git vaggits. There's a fine lot o' ash grawin 'pon top the haidge out in Vuzzy Parks, an' if I daunt git some there fer'ee, my naame wont be Wi'yum Semmens! Brave bony wauns you'll want, Missus, that'll last a mite an' thraw out some het."

"Very good, Wi'yum," her saith, "Chres'muss edn nauthen wi' out a fire, es a?"

"No, Missus," I said, "e' ednt. Tes like comin' home from Matthy's feer wi'out a maid," I saith.

Fancy you, Wi'yum, talk'ng so bold," her saith, laughing. "Time enough, I reckon, fer you to think about sparkin' et. Larn to walk afore you try to ren; an', anyhow, dawnt fer goodness sake fergit my v'irin', or you'll hear tell o't! "

Well, you, I got the firin' alright, an come Chres'muss Aive you niver seed sich a fire in your life. What a blaaze we had, to be sure! The flames shot right up droo the chimly till Mester Tervenen wus 'fraid the sparks wud catch the moothy afire. The crock, pans, an kittle, had to be drawed back fer fear they'd bust, an' the brandis just about melted. But in a little spur he wus quieter, and burnt more studdy; clear an' bright, wi the great mock all a-glowin' like the sun in July an' the ashen vaggits hissen an' splutteria like sarpints around un.

An' then the spray commenced. Mester Trevenen he sat in his big cheer to the haid o' th' table, Missus tooked tother end, an' between on wan side there wus me an' Jan Kelly, Roger Lemin an' Sol Courtice, all raced along in the green settle, while 'pon the tother side, saited 'pon a form, wus Mis' Tervenen's da'ter Nancy, Betty Quiller the sarvint maid (a Pelynter her wus), Mary Courtice, Sol's da'ter, wot did keep houze fer'n, an' Alice Tom's, the youngest maid of ol' Toms the Want-catcher auver to Polscop. My ger, wot a party 'twus! The maidens wus twitterin' an' gigglin' like a passel o heckymals, an' every whip and tich wan wud look acrost the table to we chaps, an' away to go wuss than ever. I tell ee, now, they made we feel purty bashful-like though wot they seed to laff 'bout fair puzzled me, onless twus ol' Sol, who sot glaazin like a oakweb at a big ham that wus hitched up awver the mantelpiece to smauke.

Sol had a chainey eye an, poor fella, twudnt hees fau't, o'coose, but it maade un look es if he wus allus glaazin, an gived 'ee a oncomfortable sort o' feeling when you minded it.

Now I wus some glad, after a minute er so, wi en Mester Tervenen put a stop to all this yer caper by rising up an' sayin', "Well, me frens, tes Chres'muss time, an' I opes you'll all keep it up fitty. Wi'yum, take the jar an go down to the cellar an tap th' cider. Yu knaw, me son,—the dufflyn barrel. "You may be sure I dedn't need no second askin'. Vore you could say "knife," I d a-got the jar frum th' spence, tooked the kay uv the cellar, an' was gone like winkey. My hivers, Mester, ever tasted dufflyn cider, hev'e? Tes nex' to short stuff in the way o' likker.

Well we ait an' we ait, an' we drinked an' we drinked, till poor of Sol wus glaazin' wuss than ever. Some of th' party wus bravish singers, so when somebody called fer a curl, they singed "Lo the Eastern," fine; ace, proper! Then Mester Tervenen started up, "Come and I will sing you," and tooked the solo part. Caugh, th' ol' Mester c'd sing a bit, though hes age wus aginst un a mite! After, we had blawed off steam, like, with they curls, Mester Tervenen up 'pon his feet agin an' shouted, "There, boys, that's my conterbution!— Now," he says, "everybody pay their footin': everybody sing a song, shaw a stap, or tell a story."

Lor', what a spray we had, to be sure! We maade some

21

racket; clappin'. an' stampin', an' thumpin' 'pon the table. Then after a bit we got ol' Lemin started off. Th' ol' beauty, he singed that ol' randegal, "Cornish Gels." which maade th' maidens blush, an' set mun gigglin' harder'n ever.

When my turn comed I give em "Oxen Plowin'," p'raps you knaw th' words, Mester :—"Beauty, Spark and Berry, Goodluck, Speedwell, Cherry." But when it comed to ol' Kelly to sing we had trouble to start'n. Darned if it dedn' take two extra glasses o' cider to wet his oozle 'fore he'd sing a note. When he did start he blated out, "Chase the Buffala," till you'd a thort twus a buffala roarin sure 'nuff.

Sol Courtice, pore ol' fella, gived us a fine song an' no mistake, though he's voice went a bit quavery-like, 'pon th' top notes. I can't zackly mind th'name o't but 'twus about a Bowl o' Punch an the chorus had a brave swing to un weth the words:- 'Give me th' punch ladle, an I'll fathom the bowl."

Then the maidens comed forth 'an singed together in a purty melody, while we chaps chimed in with the tenor an the bass. You can't bait that ol' song fer harmony; "Sweet Nightingale" is sweet be name an' sweet be nature.

Yer, Mester, twuz like es if that party cudden stop; waunce they wus properly set off.

Th'ol Jan Kelly acksherly got out 'pon th' floor and danced "Letterpooch," wi' a glass o' cider full to th' brim 'pon he's haid, an never spilled a drop. Tho' the toes an heels o'm wuz going clackaty-clack like a kettle-drum, he's ol' haid kipt as studdy es a waggon 'oss.

Then somebody started up "Jack Robinson"; an', well, ef anybody kin keep their feets still when they yer that— they'm deef!

But the best time of all wus when Mester Tervenen tooked

down he's ol' fiddle from the shilf an 'way we all scampe[r]ed in a dree-handed reel, singin so well es dancin' to the music, though the words es fullish:

Three-handed Reel.

"Some say th' devil's daid; buried in Fowey harbour;
Some say he's 'live agen, an 'prentice to a barber.[2]
"Tra la la la .... When Tom's father died, Tom and I took a ride, down by the river side, and home again to dinner."
Aw dear, dear, to look back pon they ol times! Tes' terrible sad, ess lay, to think all they dancers es daid en gone 'cepts Wi'yum Semmens.

I mind, out of all the maidens, there wus none that could bait Alice Toms. Lor', how that maid danced! Her feet pattered 'pon the planchen like hails dancin 'pon a linhay roof; an' light, like a feather, her wus. I'll wage' her'd skip round a piskey-ring in th' meadow an' never break th' stem of a pisky-stool in it.

Me an' Alice wus mostly partners; so et happened somehow, but there, though you'd never b'leve it to look at me, I c'd shake a leg s' well as most, Mester, 'ears agone. Coose, we chaps had to hey a spray now an' then, 'cus'

---

2. Beelzebub in the Whitehaven Mummers' Play has the lines, evidently connected with these;
"Some say the King's dead, and buried in a saucer;
Some say he's up again, and gone to be a grocer."

twad'n' like tes now, you understand, en varmplaaces after th' dayslight wus gone an' winter time fallen in, you see, an' the cows milkied, an' th' calfs fed, an' th' hosses bedded, an hay drawed in the mangers from the tallet, an' the fat bullocks maited, ther wadn't nort much left to do afore we clemmed up the temberen hill. No traapesin *er* pussivantin like young chaps looks fer now-a-days. Caugh, when I think o't I often wonder what ol' Mester Tervenen would a sed, much less thort, ef 'e c'd a seed motors, lawries, an these yer fly-be-nights moto-bikes, gwain wullagallop, waun after tother, up past he's town place!

Why th'ol' man would a bin that maazed to see 'em, he'd a scat he's haid agin the durns an' falled daid on he's awn draxel.

Well, Mester, there I be agen. 'Stead o' tellin ee 'bout Chres'muss. I've a-doddled off on some other old traade which I don't 'spose you want to hear tell nort about.

Howsomdever, I hope this yer li'l plod we've had wull a-gove 'ee sum idaya thet you b'a'nt gitting much more fun out o'life than what we poor ol' craturs ded when we wus young whipsibobs, sebenty 'ear agone.

 **Christmas on the Moor** (Cornish Dialect), by T. (North Hill). *Old Cornwall*, Vol.3, No.4, 1938.

 F.B. told me that when a boy he lived on one of the moorland farms. Those were the days when Christmas was kept up in a good old style by moorland farmers, who visited each other in turn at their parties. "I min'," said he, "ow us used to ev Chresmiss in they days. Us wud

go wan plaice, then another plaice. One plaice was at Bastreet, ole M.'s varm. E'd maike 'aste and get 'is vrashin' done, and then 'e'd get 'is barn cleared out, all ready for the party, as the varm kitchen was tu smal'. They'd range the zacks round be the walls and they'd make purty zaits, tu, tu zit on. There wud be dancin' and all zorts there gain on." He also told how once a girl who was dancing had the misfortune to dance on a rotten part of the barn floor, and it gave away. One leg went through and she found herself standing on the back of a cow beneath!

Christmas of the Yesteryears, by A. Higman. *Old Cornwall*, Vol.7, No.3, 1968.

If you are travelling on the A30 road towards Okehampton, after leaving Launceston you carry on the road until you leave a milk factory on your right. About a hundred yards further on, the road has a right hand branch. If you followed this road, you would find after a while it dwindled into a lane. After half a mile you reach a farm-gate across the road. This ended our neighbour's farm and began ours, with a gate to prevent the cattle straying. This is about half-way, and the lane gets rather muddy and rough at the end. As you reach the courtyard gate, the road goes right through the yard, with another gate at the bottom. The square house stands beside the road; the outhouses form either side, and a well at the bottom make the square courtyard. This was the isolated childhood home of my three brothers, three sisters and myself, and my eldest sister still lives there, after bringing her family up there.

Christmas began for us in October. The traveller from the Grocers into Launceston would be reeling out by memory, "Any salt, sugar, syrup, Ma'am?", when the magic words "mixed nuts, dates, spices, mixed peel" would creep in. Mother would order the extras, sometimes not delivered for two or three weeks, at such a busy time. A sack of flour would come from the Bakers and be emptied into the flour bin. We loved unpacking the groceries, to feel and smell the Christmassy items.

Each evening now was spent in stoning the raisins. We sat around the long kitchen table, with the permanent bench running around two sides of it. Occasionally we would pop a raisin in our mouth, but Dad would make us whistle or sing to put a stop to this. Soon our basins, half full of warm water, would contain most of the sticky pips, whilst the fruit was put in the large cooking bowl.

The butcher calling once a week would bring large lumps of suet, and these would chop up very finely, to have enough for the mincemeat as well; some things would go through the mincer. Mother would get out the largest milkpan, and the mixing of the puddings would begin. Each of us would solemnly have a complete stir, making a secret wish as we did so, and Dad would be brought in from whatever he was doing, to have his stir as well. All the basins were filled, and Mum, who had been hurriedly wrapping up something, pushed these small articles into the largest pudding basin. The copper was boiling. Now the pudding cloths were scalded and tied over the top of each basin, the ends in a knot for a firm grip, then all put in the copper to bubble away all day with the lovely smell seeping all through the house.

Dad would start building up the woodrick with faggots of wood and sawing the larger and thicker branches. One of us bigger ones would give a hand with the saw, and a good pile would be stored up against either side of the big hearth fire. "The holly with the most berries this year is down the branch lane, through the copse, by the river", Dad announced, and he and the boys, armed with a forked stick and a hook, would collect a large bundle, and the ends would be pushed in the earth in the front garden. The sprig that had the largest number of berries on was carefully put aside to go in the top of the Christmas pudding. It was all covered with dried grass and flower stalks, to keep the birds from eating the berries.

Now we brought out evenings our coloured rolls of crepe paper, cut them in strips and made into rings, pasted together with the flour paste we had made. Sometimes we heard of other ideas for our paper chains, and made them as well; the chains were put away until Christmas Eve.

The old lady who lived up around the corner and took some of our butter and eggs to Plymouth Market, told Mum the cases of oranges were in. They worked out at 1d. each. "Only one box, mind", Mother would say, but there would be a gross in the box, so we knew there would be plenty.

We had a grand day's shopping into Launceston now. Sometimes Dad would drive us in with the pony and trap; sometimes we would catch the train in. Mother had given us our spending money, and we each bought a present for all the family and Mum and Dad, but not on any account telling each other what we had got, and when we reached home we would hide them or pass them to Mum and Dad, who locked them away.

The next Monday, Dad announced the poultry was ready. We all put on our wrapper aprons, tied something over our hair, made up a huge hearth fire in the back kitchen, and picking commenced. Everyone, down to the smallest, sat around in a half circle, with large galvanised baths for the feathers and down. Dad kept us supplied with the birds that were killed. In those days, it was many more geese than turkeys. Chicken would come last of all—huge yellow-fleshed Indian Game chicken specially fattened.

Mother, after the first bird was picked, would stay in the other kitchen, drawing and trussing them. An apron of fat would be laid over each goose and duck, whilst the crops would be blown up with air to finish off their plump succulent appearance, and each bird laid around the stone slate slabs in the dairy.

The picking went on each and every day. The down from the geese clung like snowflakes everywhere. You were covered from head to toe and a white trail led from the shed to the house. It took two to three weeks to get through, but at last we were finished, and all the small feathers and down carefully put in clean sacks to be used for pillows and feather-beds later on. The end joint of each wing was chopped off, and the wings used as brushes for the large black stove. The giblets were scalded and peeled and put one set beside each goose. Our own goose was put aside and the giblets made into rich soup for winter evenings.

The regrators now arrived in their pony and trap, with large market baskets lined with spotless white cloths. The poultry was packed and covered with the cloths and taken out to the trap. Mum would glance proudly at Dad as she took the roll of notes for the hard work done.

It was the last week to Christmas now. Our Chapel choir met to plan the carol singing. Four of us were in the choir, and we tramped miles around most evenings, collecting for a children's home. Our limelight was the squire's house not far from the village. We would go in the mile long drive, stand on the lawns underneath the huge house where the windows were lit, and sing our hearts out. The windows would be opened, and the squire would throw us a large handkerchief with the money tied inside and wish us a "happy Christmas". We would call back "the same to you", sing another carol, then linking arms (there were about thirty of us) we would go out the drive and on to the village.

Each night it would be a different area. One night they would sing on the cobbled stones around our own back door, then on to other farms, but the last farm would always be the same one. Here they had prepared supper for us. The joy and the warmth was so welcome. As we trampled home in the frosty moonlight nights, we could see across to the distant hills. The stars were so thick in the sky. We hummed the everlasting lovely old carols. We could easily picture the angels singing in the far away distance, everything waiting for the birth of the Holy Child.

At last we reached Christmas Eve. We put up all our decorations, the holly went behind the pictures in the sitting-room, which was only used at Christmas. We got Mother to turn out all her long stockings and off we went to bed, hanging our stockings on the corner of the rails at the bottom of the bed. All those mysterious parcels the postman had been bringing would soon be disclosed. Somehow we never saw Father Christmas, but we always managed to wake long before daylight, crawl to the bottom of the bed. Our stockings were full and parcels on the bottom of the bed. We lit our candles and soon shouts of delight would follow, as we ran from room to room to show each other and Mum and Dad.

Soon we got busy. The goose was stuffed, the pudding bubbling away on the stove, mincepies were made, the extra special batch of saffron cake had been made the day before.

All was now ready. Dad sat at the head of the table and carved. The sprig of holly put in the Christmas pudding. We nearly burst having a second helping of pudding to get one of those mysterious lumps in it. Sometimes we had sixpence or even a shilling but most times a button or thimble, when our brothers would say we "would be an old maid".

The washing-up over, we would all troop to the sitting-room, where a huge fire had been burning. The gramophone was wound up. We played—mostly carols interspersed with 'Uncle Tom Cobley' and "Tavistock Goosey Fair." We played with our new toys, cracked nuts, roasted chestnuts, opened a coconut, boxes of figs, dates, chocolates, etc. and ate our orange from the toe of our Christmas stocking.

It was a late tea that day. Dad would play games with us all the evening. He taught us all the card games, and Draughts, and Dominoes. Then he would bring in a choice basket of apples from the granary, put aside for the day, and we would help ourselves.

I don't think we had a special Christmas cake in those days, but the table was covered, the best bone china used. The little ones played with their dolls, the boys with their trains, until it was finally bedtime.

We were so sleepy, we could hardly go up the stairs, but our last drowsy thought before we fell asleep would be, tomorrow would be another holiday. Oh, the magical, wonderful, beauty of Christmas!

Padstow: excerpt from: *Good Fellowship of Padstow,* by Barry Kinsmen, 2nd ed. 2011.

The Christmas Day services were always the same and began with a said celebration of the Holy Communion at seven o'clock. At about half past six the bells started their Christmas peal through the darkness of the morning. When I was confirmed, at the age of thirteen, my mother and I always attended this service. There was something very special about it. The bells had a particular message of joy. I imagined they were saying 'Christ is born in Bethlehem, Christ is born in Bethlehem' as we made our way through the darkness for dawn had not broken. The lights of the Church were already switched on when we arrived to be greeted by the sidesman with 'Happy Christmas'. In earlier times, when Mr Ravenhill's health was better, two Christmas hymns were sung at both the seven o'clock and eight o'clock Communions. The crib placed on the children's altar, was lit up and you could see from most of the church the Nativity scene. The church

31

was decorated with flowers, often chrysanthemums, and with much greenery - holly and ivy - in evidence, and also a tall Christmas tree near to the children's altar and corner. By the time the service was over, people were waiting outside for the next one, the eight o'clock Communion. The Choral Eucharist was celebrated at eleven o'clock with procession, carols and sermon, and often sung to the setting by Lloyd. The service ended with the carol 'O come all ye faithful'.

On the Sunday evening after Christmas there was always Festal Evensong when the choir sang their Christmas anthem and special carols. These were often from the *"Oxford book of Carols"* with words which seemed strange to us choirboys. 'A little child there is y' born, eia, eia'. I found the mystery of that language enthralling. The beautiful language of the liturgy and the Authorised Version had a very profound effect on me. I loved the Christmas story told by St Luke in that form which we must now call King James Version. 'And there were in the same country shepherds abiding in the fields'... 'She brought forth her first born son and laid him in the manger because there was no room in the inn'... 'The Word was made flesh and dwelt among us and we beheld his glory, the glory as of the only begotten son full of grace and truth'. How privileged I was to know and to experience the rich cadences of that version and of the beautiful collects of the Prayer Book.

There were the lovely stories I heard choir members tell while waiting in the Choir Vestry before or after service. The one that I remember best was the well known story of Johnny Fisher, the organ blower. All pipe-organs were hand pumped until the advent of electricity and Padstow Church's was no exception. The best remembered was

Johnny. He was unmarried and lived with his sisters and was probably a little simple, or 'not zackly' as we Cornish say. The most famous of his exploits happened at Christmas. The hymns for the coming Christmas carol service did not, for some reason include 'While Shepherds', which was his favourite. He made his disappointment known to Mr Ravenhill with words that have been remembered by Padstonians since the event, 'I don't care what carol you play, I'll blow "While Shepherds"'.

The Christmas Block

 M. A. Courtney. 1890.

When open chimneys were universal in farmhouses the Christmas stock, mock, or block (the log), on which a rude figure of a man had been chalked, was kindled with great ceremony; in some parts with a piece of charred wood that had been saved from the last year's "block". A log in Cornwall is almost always called a "block". "Throw a block on the fire".

Candles painted by some member of the family were often lighted at the same time.

 West Briton, 2nd February 1838.

The following is reported in an early number of the West Briton newspaper. "One evening during the Christmas of 1837 a certain Mr Lukey, of Carminow, near Helston, was sitting by the fire when his ears were suddenly assailed by cries resembling those of a child which apparently proceeded from the chimney wherein the stock lay burning, as it had been for three successive days, according to the universal custom of the country folk at this season. On examining the log he noticed that it contained a little hole, which being too small to admit his fingers he split open with an axe, only to discover to his great astonishment a large toad entombed in the centre!"

 A. K. Hamilton Jenkin. *Cornwall and its People*, 1934.

In many cases the fires of Christmas were continued until Twelfth Night or 'Old Christmas Day'. It is recorded that about the year 1830 a number of Sennen farmers assembled on this occasion at a dinner, of which one of the dishes consisted of a 'four-and-twenty blackbird pie'. After the feast, some of the boldest of the young men went out at midnight in order to see the cattle kneel, facing the east,

It would certainly appear to be more than a coincidence that these ceremonial fires of midwinter should have so nearly corresponded with the season when the sun reaches its lowest elevation at noon, and, like the bonfires of midsummer, there is reason to suppose that they owed their origin to practices far older than the Christian festival with which they had become associated.

Nick-a-Nan-Night

 West Briton, 20th January 1843.

"NICK-A-NAN-NIGHT. To the Editor of the West Briton. Sir, - I regret very much that I have so long lost sight of that number of the West Briton in which Mr. J. COUCH requested some particulars from your Newport correspondent regarding the resemblance which I thought existed betwixt the "Mari Lwyd" of Wales, and the "Nick-a-nan-Night" of Cornwall.  In conversing with a lady from Cornwall, a few days since, upon the subject, she informed me that she had seen a similar exhibition in St. Just. If this be the case, no doubt Mr. Couch will not fail to enquire into the circumstance.

The following observations may, perhaps, help Mr. C. to arrive at the conclusion I have reached, viz., that the Mari Lwyd and the Nick-a-nan-night have a common origin. The Mari Lwyd is one of the sports called sacred or religious, introduced under the highest papal authority in the middle ages. The name of the custom sufficiently and unanswerably indicates its popish origin, Mari Lwyd, or "Y fari Lwyd," literally meaning "the blessed Mary." It is a curious fact that the ancient Britons used terms signifying colour, to indicate certain states of happiness or misery - thus, Duw Gwyn, i.e. white God, meaning the blessed God; Gwynfyd, i.e. white world, meaning happiness; and there is one instance in the writings of an old bard, wherein God is called Duw Lwyd, literally grey God, meaning the venerable God. The Mari, or Mary, Lwyd, is an ambulant drama, and a distorted remnant of some old Christmas mystery of the nativity. This, although there is no direct evidence in the Welsh history of its truth, appears undeniable from the oral traditions respecting it, and the nature of the exhibition, as it always commences on Christmas-eve. The *dramatis personae* are as follows: Mary Lwyd - The Pen-ceffyl- the Conductor - Musicians, &c., Mary Lwyd is a female character, represented by a lad dressed up in woman's attire in a grotesque style, who dances and capers about to the music, and by his odd appearance never fails to occasion great amusement. The Pen-ceffyl (which signifies horse's head) is a man dressed up as nearly resembling a horse as he can, or rather the fore-part of that animal, the hind-part being omitted for convenience. The man's body forms the brisket of the horse, whilst he has attached to his shoulders a horse's head and neck finely carved, and in many cases a real horse's head. This is covered with canvass, and made so as to contain the man's arms, by which he is enabled to move about the head in imitation of the action of a horse; and generally the performer enacts his part very cleverly. By candle-light, the general period of exhibition, it has a very ghostly appearance, and produces no small dismay amongst juvenile spectators. Attached to the head of the horse is a halter, held by another man, fantastically dressed, who leads the horse, and is continually reining him in to prevent his doing mischief, though sometimes the horse is very docile, and manages to make himself very amusing. This assemblage goes about from house to house, the object being, in addition to amusement, to get beer to drink, and to collect money. The rhymes sung on the occasion are generally sung in the Welsh tongue, but their literal meaning is to this effect: The party - standing outside the door put one of their body forward to recite the challenge, or verses addressed to the inmates, and which they are to answer and excel, or the Mari Lwyd procession have a legitimate right to enter. The rhymes are rude enough, but go on to be-praise the master and mistress of the house for hospitality, and cite many good instances of the generosity of their accosters, and of the Welsh family in general, as incentives to the inmates to be profuse in their liberality on this occasion. They cite the customs of old, and wind up by saying or singing that if they are permitted to enter, "We will sing you a good song, This Christmas, this Christmas..."

The responses - and they are but seldom made - must be in reply to the few arguments the invading party have advanced, and must nullify all they have said; and thus instances have been known where a clever and intelligent native may fairly keep the Mari Lwyd out to all intents and purposes. All this is, by some intelligent persons with whom I have conversed on the subject, supposed to be the remains of the old mumming common at Christmas, and that it was originally intended - in the days of papal mystery - to represent the scene in the stable at Bethlehem; Mari Lwyd being the Virgin Mary; the Pen-ceffyl, the horses in the stable; and the man who leads the horse being Joseph. It will be seen by what I have written, that there is little reason to think my first opinion was correct, viz., that it was a druidical observance; and if the few observations I have hastily thrown together, be of any service to the talented author of the paper which gave rise to this correspondence, it will be a high gratification to. Sir, Your obedient servant, J. MARSHALL SCOTT, Newport, South Wales, January 16, 1843."

Guise Dancing

 Sandra Vingoe, Newlyn, 2012.

"Turkey Rhubarb, Turkey Rhubarb, Turkey Rhubarb I sell.
I come here from Turkey to make you all well.
Don't you all know me? Oh, me name it is Dan,
For I am the celebrated Turkey Rhubarb man."

 Up until the early 1900's the period between Christmas Day and Twelfth Night was still celebrated in West Cornwall with Guise Dancing. During this season the streets of St. Ives and the villages around Newlyn and Penzance were nightly paraded by parties of young people attired in strange costumes. In most cases the boys were dressed as girls and the girls as boys. Some of them cleverly represented historical characters; others were merely disguised with blackened faces and Nottingham lace veils, begged from their mother's meagre supply of old curtain hangings. Failing this they would mask up with scarves and bandanas covering their faces almost completely.

These 'Goose or Geese-dancers' paraded the streets and often behaved in such an unruly manner that women and children were afraid to venture out. If the doors of the houses were not locked they would enter uninvited and stay, playing all kinds of antics, until food and drink and money was given them to go away. They became such a terror to the respectable inhabitants of Penzance that the Corporation put a stop to the celebrations in about 1880. Every Christmas Eve notices were posted in conspicuous places in the town, forbidding the appearance of any dancers in the streets over the next 12 days, but they still kept up the tradition in St. Ives. Guise-dancing celebrations must have deteriorated in style since the beginning of the 19th century, as writers then spoke of a time when all enjoyed the merrymaking. Robert Hunt in his *"Popular Romances of the West of England"* published in 1870, tells us that... "...this (St Ives) is the only town in the country where the old Cornish Christmas revelry is kept up with spirit. The Guise dancing time is the twelve nights after Christmas. Guise dancing in St Ives is no more nor less than a pantomimic representation or bal masque on an extensive scale, the performers outnumbering the audience."

The Turkey Rhubarb dance always marked the finale to the evening's proceedings, after which the exhausted participants at last gave up and went home. This dance was also associated with the Christmas Mummers' play, where a concertina, sometimes referred to as a 'cordial', would provide the music. The dancers performed in heavy shoes fitted with scoots, metal pieces attached to the soles.

After a lapse during the war years several attempts were made to revive the custom in Cornish towns and villages and in some places it made a comeback. The BBC recorded and broadcast extracts from the 'Geese' dancers performance of Turkey Rhubarb in 1936 but there is no trace of it in the archives made available to researchers. Miss Helena Charles, who set up a school of inter-Celtic dancing in Cornwall in 1949, provided further corroboration of this dance as she was aware of it being used by Paul and Madron W.I. as part of their Christmas Mummers play 'St George and the Turkish Knight'.

The name 'Turkey Rhubarb' is itself a delightful enigma. There might obviously be some connection or confusion with the Turkish knight in the Mummers' Christmas play. However, Turkey Rhubarb was NOT the common garden rhubarb, parts of which are highly toxic. It was rather a Chinese herb, 'Rheum Palmatum'. Apothecaries used its root as a cure for diarrhoea, but its use can cause intense cramping. Larger doses were employed as a laxative. Morton Nance's *Cornish Dictionary* gives 'Tavol Turkey' is an alternative Cornish word for Rhubarb. Perhaps the antics of the dancers were akin to the cramps effect on the body and someone made the humorous [?] connection.

The dance is in fact a form of mazurka, a polish peasant dance which spread westwards across Europe during the late eighteenth century. It seems to be found in most European dancing traditions and dancers in Champagne, Holland, Brittany and Ireland have performed recognisable variants. By far the closest to the Cornish is that done on the West coast of Ireland variously called 'Father Murphy's Topcoat' or 'Patsy Heeny'. Although this is as Irish in style as ours is Cornish the two dances are almost interchangeable.[3] Now, where did I put they old net curtens?

The Cornish Christmas Bush

In Cornwall the tradition of hanging up the "Bush" goes back to a pagan festival celebrating the Winter Solstice.

The construction of the bush is a memento of the practice of human sacrifice practiced by the Celts before the coming of Christianity. Great cages of withies were fashioned in the likeness of the gods and into these human victims were crowded and at midnight on the solstice eve they would be burnt as an offering to the solar deity in order that he might furnish the god with renewed power to

---

3. Dee Brotherton's efforts to revive the ancient Guizing' tradition at Christmas are fully supported by St Ives OCS and in 2009 the dance was performed once again. However, these days many doors to the cottages at 'Downalong' will remain firmly locked, but that will not bother those joining in the celebrations.

rejuvenate the soil. So the "Bush", just like the Hobby Hoss (which in tradition was also made of withies), is a celebration of the coming of the sun god and new life. With the introduction of Christianity the tradition was adapted by the first Christian missionaries who just like the Bards before them would cut Holly, Ivy and Mistletoe bushes using a bronze sickle and then bless the cuttings before handing them to the people who would take them home to make the bush. Now the bush was used to celebrate the new life that had come with the birth of the baby Jesus. So like many of the old traditions yet another was used by the church as a way of letting the people continue to use the old practice of their new faith.

Use willow canes to make two hoops. Fasten these one inside the other to make a ball shape. Decorate the hoops with Holly, Ivy and Mistletoe which were believed by the old ones to have magical powers as they stayed green when everything around them was dying. Wrap the holly and the ivy around the hoops and fasten an apple inside the top and hang the mistletoe below the hoops.

On Solstice eve the 20th of December, secure the bush to the ceiling and taking great care, fasten a red candle inside the bush and light just before midnight then form a ring and dance under the bush welcoming the rebirth of the God of Light. Make sure you extinguish the candle before leaving the room.

The Christmas Bush, by Gladys Hunkin. *Old Cornwall*, Vol.6, No.12, 1967.

If there is one experience more joyous than returning home at Christmas it is to be there to welcome a loved one after a long absence. I close my eyes and see my brother and two sisters and myself racing to meet my father home from his ship. Memory revives the fresh sea-scent he brought with him for, as Kipling says, "Smells are surer than sounds and sights to make the heart-strings crack." Once more he had arrived for Christmas in time to make for us the Cornish Bush an old custom, depicted in Mordon's drawing.

The Bush, known much earlier than the Victorian Christmas tree, was made by interlinking two wooden hoops at right angles and tying them firmly together; the hollow globe of four curves thus formed was covered in twists of red crinkled paper and decorated along the staves with holly, ivy or other evergreens. I do not recollect mistletoe, though I have heard it called "The Kissing Bough." Fruit such as red apples and oranges was added, and the sparkling shining balls unknown in earlier days. Our presents also adorned the dainty structure which was hung in a window. One red candle inside at the base was lit after dark, and I recall this once caused a near-tragedy by setting the whole thing ablaze—no candle after that! I believe we thought the light welcomed the Infant Christ on his way to Bethlehem.

When I returned to my native county I made one of these bushes and was asked ironically if it signified "RIP, the Spirit of Christmas!" Another I made for a church bazaar was received with curiosity and interest.

I shall place Mordon's beautiful drawing with other nostalgic treasures - the naval button, the wisp of my mother's dark hair, with no trace of grey, cut on her golden wedding, the dried scrap of Cornish heather... I now embalm them all afresh with this recollection of a happy childhood.

FOOD & DRINK

Christmas Food

 Royal Cornwall Gazette, 18th December 1875.

To be Sold

FOR YOUR CHRISTMAS GROCERIES

GO TO

J. C. CRAPP'S

CHURCH LANE, TRURO

Flour 17½ lbs. 2s 5d.

Lemon Peel 8d per lb.

Lump Sugar 3s 9d per doz.

New Currants 4d per lb.

Raisins 4½d per lb.

Muscatels 10d to 16d per lb.

Broad Figs 2d per lb.

Soap 3½ lbs for 10d

Good Rice 1½d per lb.

Orange and other fruits

Royal Cornwall Gazette, 18th December 1875.

A TREAT

Christmas Cases

WILL contain Cognac Brandy, Jamaica Rum, Gin, Whiskey, Geneva, Sherry, Port, Marsala, Madeira, Malaga, Sparkling Moselle, Hock, Burgundy, and Champagne, Sauterne, Claret, Chablis, Orange Brandy, Cherry Brandy, Ginger Brandy, Milk Punch, Lovage, Curacao, Vermouth, Noyan, Orange Bitters , Shrub, Mint, Gingerette, Cloves, &c, guaranteed pure.

AN ASSORTMENT OF 12 BOTTLES

(left to the choice of the purchaser)

AND A PACKET OF CIGARS

FOR 36s.

Carriage paid to any railway station in Cornwall.

R. Easton Thomas and Co.

WHOLESALE WINE, SPIRIT, ALE & PORTER
MERCHANTS

FALMOUTH

That Real Ambrosia. From: John Trenhaile. *Dolly Pentreath and other Humorous Cornish Tales in Verse,* 1854.

That real ambrosia (not a poet's dream)
Food for celestials, Cornwall's clotted cream?
Ye eastern epicures who rack your brain,
And earth explore, rich viands to obtain,

To Cornwall haste; your search will then be o'er;
Once taste our cream;—you'll sigh for nothing more.
O never think of Italy or France!
Health, turbot, cream, await you at Penzance.

And many a pie she brought (her country's boast)
Surpassing far all boiled meat and roast
Of making pies no wonder she was proud,
Her skill was universally allowed.

Ingredients various she, with art employed;
Pilchards and cream she most of all enjoyed;
Potatoes, leeks, and turnips oft would meet,
With bacon laid between, in concord sweet;

Onions and apples made a summer dish,
O'erlaid with mutton, fat as heart could wish;
Parsley and spinach, joined with fish or veal,
With luscious cream, she thought indeed genteel.

Old Christmas had his own sweet giblet pie,
Which with the first of luxuries may vie
A goose's giblets, apples, figs and spice,
Beef, mutton, onions, pork and currants nice,

With salt and pepper seasoned, form the treat,
Which none, who once could taste, would cease to eat,
There runs a tale (I only hope it's true):
The Devill his face would ne'er in Cornwall show.

He once to Plymouth came upon a tour,
Or Devonport (I am not very sure);
And, having a few leisure days to spend,
Purposed a journey to the far Land's-end

But, ere he crossed the ferry, news was brought,
The Cornish, of his trip, advice had got,
And had assembled in a powerful band,
And swore he never on their coast should land

Or, if he did, their prowess all would try,
To kill the wretch and put him in a pie!
His highness, therefore, never ventured down,
But hurried back, with railway speed, to town.

When looking at the subject of Christmas food and drink in Cornwall we must start with Butter and Cream after all, without these, what would Christmas be.

H.P. Olivey. *History of the Parish of Mylor*, 1907.

There are various customs and usages, which are peculiarly Cornish, these from time immemorial have been observed in the parish of Mylor. For instance, the process of the dairy. Who would think of making butter without first "scalding" the milk? And even in recent times, since the introduction of the "separator", the cream is still "scalded". This was an ancient British practice, and is peculiar to this county and part of Devon. This process, like many we read of in Holy Scripture of the Jewish hygienic laws, has anticipated modern science by sterilizing the milk and destroying the noxious germs, and is said to have been introduced by the Phoenicians, who at a very early date traded with this county for tin.

The process of this "scalding" is to allow the milk twelve or twenty-four hours for the cream to rise on the surface, and then to place the pans containing it over the fire in a kettle containing hot water, and allow it to remain until sufficiently warmed throughout. It is then allowed to cool and the cream skimmed off. The butter made from this has certainly better keeping qualities than that made from the unprepared cream.

I find many allusions to this "clotted" or clouted cream. Polwhele says: "I doubt not that of our cream was made the very sort of butter so much esteemed by the Romans. Butter was a British luxury with which the Romans were unacquainted "; and, quoting Mrs. Bray (*Borders*, II, p. 34), "Of what an ancient date your scalded cream is you little think," said I to a good old dairy-woman. 'Auntient,' she exclaimed, 'I'se warrant he's as old as Adam; for all the best things in the world were to be had in Paradise."

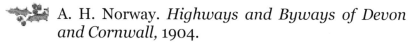 A. H. Norway. *Highways and Byways of Devon and Cornwall*, 1904.

Nothing on earth or in our poet's dream
Is so rich and rare as your Cornish Cream
Its orient tinge like spring time morn,

Or baby buttercups newly born;
Its barmy perfume, delicate pulp,
One longs to swallow it all at a gulp,
Sure man had ne'er such gifts or theme
As your melt-in-the-mouthy Cornish cream.

Pies

 R. Polwhele. *The Old English Gentleman, a Poem*, 1797.

The following has reference to cream with the famous Cornish pies:

Dear to Cornish palates, one and all,
Appeas'd in crusted pomp to grace the hall,
The pye, where herbs with veal in union meet,
The tasteful parsley, the nutritious beet,
The bitter mercury wild, nor valued less
The watery lettuce and the pungent cress;
When ravishing with odours every nose,
The leek o'er layers of the pilchard rose,
Or, in a gentler harmony,with pork,
Ere yet of mouths it claim'd the playful work,
Attack'd the nostril with a tempting steam,
As opening, it ingulph'd the golden cream.

 William King, in his *Art of Cookery*, 1708, gives us some strange combinations:

"Trotter from quince and apples first did frame
A Pye, which still retains his proper name,
Tho' common grown, yet with white sugar strew'd
And buttered well, its goodness is allow'd."
"Our fathers most admir'd their sauces sweet,
And often ask'd for sugar with their meat;

They butter'd currants on fat veal bestow'd,
And Rumps of Beef with Virgin Honey strow'd."

 M. A. Courtney. 1890.

A sweet giblet pie was one of the standing dishes at a Christmas dinner - a kind of mince-pie, into which the giblets of a goose, boiled and finely chopped, were put instead of beef. Cornwall is noted for its pies, that are eaten on all occasions; some of them are curious mixtures, such as:

Squab-pie, which is made with layers of well-seasoned fat mutton and apples, with onions and raisins.

Mackerel pie: the ingredients of this are mackerel and parsley stewed in milk, then covered with a paste and baked. When brought to table a hole is cut in the paste, and a basin of clotted cream thrown in.

Muggetty pie, made from sheep's entrails (muggets), parsley, and cream.

There is a local saying that "The devil is afraid to come into Cornwall for fear of being baked in a pie."

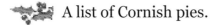 A list of Cornish pies.

•Squab pie, made with young pigeons (now made with mutton - see below).

•Nattlin pie, made with pigs' entrails, "chit'lins".

•Muggety pie, made with sheep's entrails, parsley and cream.

•Fishy pie.

•Likkey pie, made with Leeks and boiled eggs.

•Conger pie, made with the Conger Eel.

•Tetty pie. Made with potatoes, onions and left over roast or boiled meat.

•Parsley pie.

•Giblet pie. (See below).

•Herby pie, made with nettles, peppercorns, parsley, mustard, spinach, & pork.

•Tiddago pie, made with prematurely born 'veers' or suckling pigs.

•Lamby-pie, made with very young lambs that have been overlaid.

•Bottom pie.

•Piggy pie.

•Sour sop pie, made with Sorrell.

•Starry gazey pie, made with seven sorts of fish.

Giblet Pie

Duck or Goose Giblets 450g (1lb)
Rump Steak 1
Onion 1
Bunch Savoury Herbs ½ tsp
Whole Black Pepper
Plain Crust

Clean and put the giblets into a saucepan with an onion, whole pepper and a bunch of savoury herbs.

Add just over a pint of water and simmer gently for about 1½ hour.

Remove the giblets, let them cool and cut them into pieces. Strain the liquor.

Line the bottom of a pie dish with a few pieces of steak.

Add a layer of giblets and a few more pieces of steak.

Season with salt and pepper, pour in the liquor.

Cover with a plain crust and bake for rather more than 1 hour in a brisk oven.

Cover a piece of paper over the pie, to prevent the crust taking too much colour.

Time: 1½ hour to stew the giblets, about 1 hour to bake the pie.

Sufficient for 5 or 6 persons.

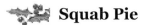 Squab Pie

Cornish Notes and Queries, 1ˢᵗ series, 1906.

In the old days Squab-pie was deemed luxurious beyond all other pies. The recipe for it has been given by an unknown writer in verse, as follows:

Of wheaten walls erect your paste;
Let the round mass expand its breast.
Next slice your apples cull'd so fresh,
Let the fat sheep supply its flesh,
Then add an onion's stinging juice -
A sprinkling – be not too profuse
Well mix't, these nice ingredients, sure,
Might gratify an epicure!

The Cornish Christmas Minced Pie.

The Cornish Christmas minced pie was oblong in shape, in imitation of the manger where our Saviour was laid. The following recipe is recorded as having been handed down in the same family for generations.

A pound of beef suet chopped fine,
A pound of currants,

A pound of raisins,
A pound of apples,
Two or three eggs,
And allspice.

All beat very fine and sweetened to taste, a little salt, and as much brandy and wine as you like.

Other dishes

 **Raw Fry**

Contributed by Sandra Pritchard, *née* Vingoe.

This is a Recipe for a dish that has been eaten and enjoyed by my family and lots of others from the Penwith area for many years. "Raw Fry" as it is known is a substantial but cheap dish to eat on cold winter days and was a favourite in the days after Christmas when bacon from the Christmas pig was plentiful.

Ingredients for two people

Three large potatoes
Four rashers of smoked bacon
One ounce of dripping
Salt and pepper
One teaspoon of cornflower
Vinegar

Method

Peel and slice potatoes quite thin.

Cut bacon into large pieces.

Heat dripping (or oil) in frying pan and add bacon.

Cook until sealed then remove bacon from pan.

Put the sliced potatoes into the pan and seal in the hot fat and bacon juices.

Add the bacon and salt and pepper to taste.

Cover with water and leave to cook on a low heat until the potatoes are cooked and just starting to break up.

Add one teaspoon of cornflower and thicken.

Serve hot with bread and butter adding a dash of vinegar to taste.

 Hog's Pudding

Contributed by Marge Parrill.

3 1/2 lbs ground pork
3/4 cup dried bread crumbs
1/2 tsp pepper
3/4 tsp salt
1/2 tsp garlic powder
1/8 tsp ground cumin
1/8 tsp celery powder
1/8 tsp ground oregano
1/2 tsp onion powder
Sausage sized casings

Place ingredients in a large bowl and mix.

Stuff casings with the mixture (a great deal of work).

Tie the bottom when you have the amount that you want and repeat until all the mixture is used.

Cut and boil until done. Yum, yum.

Christmas Drinks

 Royal Cornwall Gazette, 1ˢᵗ December 1821.

FRENCH WINES
By order of the Honorable Commissioners of
His Majesty's Excise and Customs.

On Wednesday the 5ᵗʰ day of December next, at eleven
o'clock in the forenoon will be SOLD BY AUCTION at the
Star Inn, in the Borough of St Ives, as much as Thirty Casks
of
FRENCH RED & WHITE WINE
(DUTY FREE)
Lately picked up at sea, as will amount to £300, the sum
allowed for the salvage thereof.
The wines are of excellent quality, and fit for particular
consumption.
For further information, apply to the Officers of the Customs
and Excise, at St Ives, or to
MR. ALEXANDER MARRACK
Of Penzance, Auctioneer
Dated 22ⁿᵈ November , 1821.

 Cornish Mead, by William Bottrell.

The old method of making mead, or metheglin, in West
Cornwall was to put four pounds of honey to one gallon of
water; boil it one hour, skim it well, then add one ounce of
hops to every gallon, and boil it half-an-hour longer, and
let it stand till next day. Put it into your cask or bottles. To
every gallon add a gill of brandy; stop it lightly till the
fermentation is over; then stop it very loose. Keep it one
year before you tap. More recently the old ladies who were
noted for making good mead (or sweet-drink as they call

it), boiled the combs from which the honey had been drained until all the honey that remained was extracted. They then strained it, and added as much more honey as made the drink strong enough to float an egg. To every gallon they added one ounce of cloves; the same of allspice; half-an-ounce of coriander; the same weight of caraway-seed.

 Sometimes cinnamon and mace were used instead of the seeds. Others, who preferred the flavour and perfume of aromatic plants, boiled in the water, before they added the honey, the tops of sweet-briar, flowers of thyme, rosemary, sweet marjoram, or any other sweet herbs they liked; then finished as above.

Eggy-hot

At the plentiful supper always provided on this night, egg-hot, or eggy-hot, was the principal drink. It was made with eggs, hot beer, sugar, and rum, and was poured from one jug into another until it became quite white and covered with froth.

12 egg yolks
5 cloves, whole
8 cups beer
3 cups light rum
1¾ cups sugar
2½ teaspoons vanilla essence
1 teaspoon cinnamon, ground
¾ teaspoon nutmeg, ground

Pour beer into a saucepan over low heat and blend in the cloves, cinnamon and half a teaspoon of the vanilla essence.

Keep stirring while mixture heats, and remove from heat just before boiling point.

Now mix the sugar and all the egg yolks in a bowl. whisking them well so that they are light and fluffy.

Gently a little at a time, pour in the beer mixture while continuing to whisk.

Transfer mixture back into your saucepan over a medium heat while continuing to stir. Never let the mixture reach boiling point!!

Keep stirring until your Eggy-hot mixture starts to resemble custard.

Pour and strain the mixture into a jug, making sure to remove the cloves.

Gently stir in the light rum, remaining vanilla and ground nutmeg.

Then pour mixture from one jug to the other until the mixture is nice and frothy.

This should be enough for 8 people.

Blackberry Warmer - Winter Drink

This drink comes from an old Penzance recipe and was a favourite drink with both adults and children. In the summer the lanes and hedgerows would be searched for the finest blackberries which would be turned into a drink for Christmas.

Ingredients

6 cups blackberries
1 pint vinegar

6 cloves for every pint of juice

1/2 inch piece root ginger for every pint of juice

2 cups sugar for every pint of juice

Method

Soak the blackberries in the vinegar for 24 hours.

Strain and add the cloves, sugar and ginger to the juice.

Boil for half an hour.

Strain and bottle.

Other Beverages

Here are three very old recipes which they only give in rather LARGE measures... "Shows 'ow common the 'ole stuff was in they there parts, yew never knawed what t' do wid'n all."

 Sloe Gin

Geneva Gin was a staple part of the smuggling trade in Cornwall. On February 10th 1805 the H.M. Customs seized a thousand gallons of Brandy, Rum and Geneva from local smugglers at Sennen. The smugglers put up a fight and shots were fired. A Sennen man John George was captured, tried and sentenced to hang for the offence at the Old Bailey on the 24th April 1805.[4]

Recipe

Pick two litres of sloes from blackthorn hedges in October or November making sure they are ripe.

Separate two litres of gin into four litre bottles.

---

4. Old Bailey Records Reference Number: t18050424-38

Having washed the sloes cut or prick them and drop a quarter of your crop into each bottle. This should bring the gin almost to the top.

Now add 150g of sugar to each bottle and put the stopper on.

All you have to do now is gently shake each bottle each day for the first week then weekly for two months. It is now ready to drink so open one bottle and try it. Then put the rest away until Christmas when it will taste even better.

Shrub Cordial

Take two quarts of brandy and put into a large bottle and put into that the juice of five lemons, the peels of two lemons plus half a nutmeg.

Stop it up and let it stand for three days and then add to it, three pints of white wine, a pound and a half of sugar: mix it and strain it twice through a flannel and bottle it up.

"'Tis a pretty wine and a cordial".

For each tot of rum add a double tot of shrub.

At the end of the evening everyone was cordial!

Orange Shrub

The recipe for Orange Shrub had even more largesse.

"Break one hundred pounds of loaf sugar into small pieces, put it into twenty gallons of water, boil it till the sugar is melted, skim it well and put into a tub to cool: when cold, put it into a cask, with thirty gallons of good Jamaica rum, and fifteen gallons of orange juice [mind to strain all the seeds out of the juice] mix them well together; then beat up the whites of six eggs very well, stir them well in, let it stand a week to fine, and then draw it off for use."

There is an estimate that each year around the 1780's brandy alone was smuggled at the rate of six bottles per head of the adult population.

In 1785 Cognac, the very finest brandy was exported to Britain at an estimated 1,100,000 gallons and in addition Jamaican rum came cheap from the slave plantations of the West Indies.

No wonder at Christmas they sang "God Rest Ye Merry Gentlemen".

Brandy for Christmas.

West Briton, 27th December 1839.

On Saturday morning, Mr. H. C. Turner, and Mr. Edmund Randall, two vigilant and active officers, the first of the Excise, and the other of the Customs, having some cause to suspect that contraband goods were brought into town by the stage vans coming from St. Austell, Tregony, and other places near the south coast, took their station about a mile out, on the eastern turnpike road, and carefully searched all the vans as they arrived. Among these was one belonging to a man called Nicholas Fugler, of Tregony, in which they found a keg of French brandy, concealed in a hamper with a little straw on top of it. Upon this they seized the van and all it contained, together with the van horse, and drove off to the Customs house, carrying Fugler with them in custody.

The Christmas and the Dilly

Geo. C. Boase. *Notes and Queries*, 5th series, 21st December 1878.

In some parts of the country it is customary for each household to make a batch of currant cakes on Christmas-eve. These cakes are made in the ordinary manner, coloured with saffron, as is the custom in these parts. On this occasion the peculiarity of the cakes is, that a small portion of the dough in the centre of each top is pulled up and made into a form which resembles a very small cake on the top of a large one, and this centre-piece is usually called "the Christmas". Each person in the house has his or her especial cake, and every person ought to take a small piece of every other person's cake. Similar cakes are also bestowed on the hangers-on of the establishment, such as laundresses, seamstresses, charwomen, &c.; and even some people who are in the receipt of weekly charity call, as a matter of course, for their Christmas cakes. The cakes must not be cut until Christmas-day, it being probably "unlucky to eat them sooner". The materials to make these and nearly all the cakes at this season were at one time given by the grocers to their principal customers.

J. Kelynack. *Old Cornwall,* Vol.5, No.10, 1959.

As far back as I can remember, I with all the other members of our family had a special bun, made in the shape of a bird, to eat on Christmas Eve. My Mother and her brothers, and their parents, uncles and aunts had always done the same. My great-grandparents, when the Christmas saffron cake was being made, used to pick out pieces of the dough, make them into this bird-shape and bake them. Then each member of the family was given one and the dilly carol was sung (see Carol section). My sister gave such buns to her children and my niece, who lives with me, says, "Yes, I remember that lovely bird".

Cornish Saffron Cake

Day 1: Preparing the saffron.

Half a teaspoon of saffron strands (purchase from a chemist).

Half a cup milk and water combined.

Boil the half-cup of the milk and water mix and cut the saffron into very fine strands.

Next place the strands in a glass jug and pour the boiling milk and water over it. Cover and leave to steep overnight.

Day 2: You will now need the following ingredients:

Another half- cup of milk and water combined
500g unbleached white bread flour
1 teaspoon fine sea salt
150g butter (cut into small chunks)
50g light muscovado sugar
15g fresh yeast
100g mixed fruit

Preheat oven to 180C/350F/Gas 4.

Grease a suitable-sized loaf tin.

Put fresh yeast into a small bowl with a teaspoon of sugar and half a cup of warm milk and water (make sure it is not too hot or it will kill the yeast).

Rub fat into the flour until the mixture resembles fine breadcrumbs.

Stir in sugar.

When yeast has risen in the cup, make a pit in the center of the flour mixture and pour in the yeast, covering with a sprinkle of flour.

When this mixture cracks and the yeast 'sponges' through, warm the previously steeped saffron mixture a little and add this to the mix, together with the mixed fruit. Combine using your hand to make a soft (but not sticky) dough (add a little more liquid at this stage, if required).

Turn out onto a very lightly floured surface and knead for about 5 minutes.

Cover with a clean tea towel and leave in a warm place to rise (usually about 30-45 minutes).

Put into the greased loaf tin, cover and leave to rise again until it is level with the top of the tin (about 1 hr).

Bake for 45mins to 1 hr. Leave to cool on a wire rack.

The above recipe can be made into buns and baked for approx 20 mins.

A little grated nutmeg is sometimes added to the recipe.

Dried yeast can be used (approx 7g) - please refer to instructions on package and adapt method accordingly.

G. C. Boase. *Reminiscences of Penzance*, 1883.

Ginger cakes and biscuits were popular treats on many festive occasions.

We used to like some flat cakes of gingerbread, marked in four squares with a raisin in each square. The names of these were, in schoolboy literature, "lillybangers".

Honey Combed Gingerbread

St Ives Weekly Summary & Visitors List, 27th December 1890.

Put four ounces of fresh butter into a jar, near the fire, with half a pound of treacle, and half a pound of moist sugar.

Mix half a pound of flour with one teaspoonful of ground ginger, the finely chopped rind and juice of half a lemon, and one teaspoonful of powdered cinnamon.

When the butter is melted, mix it with the treacle &c., into the flour, and beat all together for some minutes.

Spread the mixture thinly upon baking tins and bake in a moderate oven. Watch it particularly as soon as the ginger-bread is done enough, take it out, cut it into squares and curl each square round the finger.

Keep close covered in a tin box. This ginger-bread will keep for three to four weeks, but is best when newly made.

Should it lose its crispness, it should be put into the oven for two or three minutes before being used.

Time 10 minutes to bake. Probable cost 10d [1890 prices] for this quantity.

 **Ginger Fairings**

<u>Ingredients</u>

8oz flour
½ tsp bicarbonate of soda
4oz butter or margarine
1½ tsp baking powder
4oz granulated sugar
½ tsp cinnamon
4oz golden syrup (approx. 2 tbsp)
1 tsp ground ginger
1 tsp mixed spice
Pinch salt

<u>Method</u>

Sift together the dry ingredients.

Rub in the butter or margarine.

Add the syrup and mix together well, to a smooth pliable paste, not too wet, not too dry.

With the hand, roll the mixture into a long roll.

Cut off small sections and shape into balls.

Place these on a greased baking tray, leaving plenty of room for spreading.

Heat the oven to 400°F, 200°C, Gas Mark 6. Bake on the top shelf until golden (about 7 minutes), then on a lower shelf to drop and spread for 5 minutes.

 **Chirky Wheeler**

Aptly named Chirky Wheeler - 'chirks' is an old Cornish dialect word for cinders from the fire. The Chirky Wheeler was made by first dragging the chirks into the middle of the hearth then adding grigglins (small twigs and branches) to create the heat to a flat iron plate which was placed on top of them. Whilst this was getting hot the following were mixed:

1 lb flour
6 oz currants
8 oz butter
pinch salt
milk to mix

Rub fat roughly into flour - do not mix too finely (i e leave fat as small pieces in the mix) as the dough needs to be a little 'flakey'. Add currants and a pinch of salt and bind together with milk. Roll mixture into a thin cake and place on the baker. Turn as necessary, like a pancake, to ensure it is thoroughly cooked through and golden brown (or slightly burnt!) on the outside.

The dish Chirky Wheeler was a favourite on cold winter days and was easy to make when unexpected visitors arrived. For a sweeter version you must add 2 oz. of sugar to the ingredients.[5]

M. A. Courtney. 1890.

All Christmas cakes must be eaten by the night of Twelfth-tide, as it is unlucky to have any left, and all decorations must be taken down on the next day, because for every forgotten leaf of evergreen a ghost will be seen in the

---

5. Today a frying pan can be used instead of the Baker.

house in the coarse of the ensuing year. The latter superstition does not prevail, however, in all parts of Cornwall, as in some districts a small branch is kept to scare away evil spirits.

Market Reports

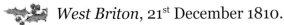 *West Briton*, 21ˢᵗ December 1810.

Figs for Sale: About 900 frails of Figs just landed from Lisbon and are in excellent order.
Francis S. Symonds (Merchant) Falmouth.

Truro. Thomas Allom, c.1830

 West Briton, 28ᵗʰ December 1837.

Truro Market: Our meat market on Saturday last did not present so fine an appearance, as it is usual on Christmas occasions. The general character of the beef, though good, being far from what is usually dominated prime. The poultry market was however, well supplied, the Geese especially being numerous and fine; but in consequence of the smallness of the room, the heat occasioned by the dense crowd was so great that the fat on some of them was literally melting and the inconvenience to both buyers and sellers was almost insufferable.

Redruth. Rock & Co., 1858.

West Briton, 24th December 1877.

Turkeys: On Monday about 300 Turkeys were brought to the Redruth Railway Station. Each bird was weighed and ticketed at the Market Place which attracted a great crowd. The birds were in fine condition.

West Briton, 30th December 1842.

Launceston Christmas Market: The show of meat at the Launceston Christmas market was, if possible, more excellent than on any former occasion. The bullock fed by

F. RODD, Esq., and killed by Mr. BARTLETT, did great credit to both feeder and butcher. An excellent bullock was also killed by Mr. SPENCER, fed by J. DOIDGE, Esq., but among so much excellence it is almost invidious to particularise.

Feeding the Poor at Christmas

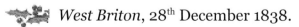 *West Briton*, 28th December 1838.

Chacewater: On Saturday last, Matthew Moyle, Esq., of Chacewater, gave his annual donation of Ten Pounds to the poor widows of that place; in addition to which this truly philanthropic gentleman distributed during the past week betwixt Twenty and Thirty Pounds, to the poor families of his neighbourhood. On Monday, the inhabitants of Chacewater distributed one hundred bushels of coal among the poor.

St Austell: On Monday last, the carcases of two fine bullocks and six sheep, weighing together more than 3000 lbs., were distributed in upwards of 600 huts among the poor of the parish of St. Austell, the munificent donation of Sir J. S. G. Sawle, Bart., of Penrice; and on Christmas-day, the poor in the workhouse were plentifully regaled with beef and plum-pudding, partly the gift of the Hon. Bart.

Antony and Sheviock: Seven hundred weight of beef, with a proportionate quantity of bread, have been this week distributed to the poor by the order of W. P. Carew, Esq., of Antony House. Orders have also been given by the Earl of Mount Edgcumbe for the distribution of the usual Christmas donations of meat, bread, and clothing.

 West Briton, 2ⁿᵈ January 1846.

Illogan: Lady BASSET caused two fat bullocks to be slaughtered on Christmas eve, and distributed together with several sacks of flour, among the poor of the parish of Illogan.

Helston: Philip Vyvian Robinson, Esq., late of Nansloe, but now of Tehidy, has ordered to be distributed among (as he calls them) his poorer neighbours at the top of Meneage-street, Helston, a large quantity of coals.

South Petherwin: W. A. H. Arundell, Esq., of Trebursye House, near Launceston, generously distributed a large quantity of blankets last week, among the poor of South Petherwin.

Lawhitton: George W. Webber, Esq., of Hexworthy House, Launceston, last week, made his annual presentation of beef, bread, and wood, to the poor families of the parish of Lawhitton.

Saint Stephens Coombe, in Branwell: The week before last, the cottage labourers of Saint Stephens Coombe, in Branwell, slaughtered their twelve months old pigs against Christmas. Although the pigs, amounting to 29 in number, were not well fed, in consequence of the scarcity of potatoes, yet the whole lot together weighted 11,397 pounds, thus averaging 19 score and 13 pounds to each pig. In estimating the expense of feeding this year, it was found to be much greater than that of last year.

West Briton, 31ˢᵗ December 1847.

SEASONABLE LIBERALITY - On Friday last, upwards of seven hundred pounds of beef and a large quantity of bread was distributed amongst one hundred and sixty poor families residing in the neighbourhood of Menabilly; and one guinea and warm clothing and bedding to each of twenty poor widows occupying the Rashleigh alms houses at Fowey and Tywardreath, being the annual munificent gift of WILLIAM RASHLEIGH, Esq., Menabilly.

West Briton, 7ᵗʰ January 1848.

Falmouth: On Wednesday last, tea &c. was provided at the Sailors' Room, Falmouth, by some unknown friend to the aged poor of that town. The entertainment was conducted by a committee of young ladies, each of whom took a table, and about one hundred and fifty elders were regaled with the abundance set forth. The sight was most imposing, and the smiling poor welcomed the new year of 1848. After the cloth was removed, the REV. T.

WILDBORE (Independent minister) addressed the company in a most suitable and impressive manner, whilst all present appeared deeply affected.

St. Columb Union House: The inmates of this house were on Christmas day plentifully supplied with an excellent dinner of roast beef, beer, and plum pudding; and on New Year's day were again regaled with cake and tea. All seemed much pleased and the poor are very grateful to those kind friends who contributed so liberally to their entertainment. Much praise is also due to Mr. and Mrs. BAYLY for the good order and management observed in serving out the dinner and tea.

St. Austell Union: The inmates of the Union House were regaled on Christmas day with old English fare, the gift of the Guardians, and again on New Year's day the gift of J. H. TREMAYNE, Esq.

Mawgan & St Martin and Helston: On Christmas eve two large oxen were slaughtered by order of SIR R. R. VYVYAN, Bart., of Trelowarren, and distributed to the poor of Mawgan and St. Martin parishes, and also £5 in money, a portion of which was sent to the Helston union-house, and distributed among those who were natives of the above parishes; in addition to which a great number of blankets and other clothing have been distributed among the necessitous poor, in several adjoining parishes.

West Briton, 11th April 1851.

The Mousehole Fishermen: A correspondent writes as follows: The poverty with which the fishermen of Mousehole are at this time contending, cannot but be apparent to the most casual observer. Although some kind friend, within the last ten days, has supplied the wants of a few, still the main bulk of the people are in the most abject poverty, and the scarcity of fish on the coast seems to bode some dreadful deprivations. The fishermen have been industriously trying since Christmas, but I may say that during that time some of them have not earned the bread they have eaten, and I doubt not that many, through a delicacy of feeling to have their cases known, have felt all the severities of poverty. I trust that some kind friends will commiserate the case of these thrifty, but poor people, and endeavour to mitigate the calamity under which they are suffering, and grant them that timely aid which they so much stand in need of.

 West Briton, December 1876.

Cornwall Lunatic Asylum: The patients of the CLA were regaled on Christmas Day with an abundance of roast Geese and Pork, Plum Pudding Etc.

 West Briton, 27th December 1877.

Fowey: Seasonable Benevolence - The poor residing in the parishes adjacent to Menabilly received on Christmas Eve, the usual supply of beef and bread for their Christmas dinners. Every poor person received one shilling each.

Truro: On Christmas-day, the poor in Truro workhouse were treated with a dinner of roast beef and plum pudding, and a pint of beer each, which had been kindly provided by the private subscription of the gentlemen composing the board of guardians. Seventy-two persons sat down to dinner, the average of whose ages was upwards of 70 years. The inmates of Probus workhouse had a similar treat.

Falmouth: On Christmas day, the poor in the town and parish work-house at Falmouth, were regaled with roast beef and plum pudding, in the presence of several ladies and gentlemen who went to see them partake of their treat. The fare was of the best description, and an extra allowance was given to each individual.

Redruth Union House: The inmate paupers of this union were enabled to celebrate the Christmas in the most approved old English manner. The governor's family, consisting of 33 men, 120 women, and 150 children, after attending the chapel, in which service was performed by the REV. J. W. HAWKSLEY, sen., sat down to a dinner which very few gentlemen would wish to have to pay for every day - veritable mountains of beef and plum pudding, and streams of beer; beef of the best cuts, and plum pudding that really deserved to be called by that very respectable appellation, and not the mere lock jaw dumplings which, too frequently for the inmates of union-houses, usurp the honourable title. The paupers "ate and were filled", and were SATISFIED, moreover, and very grateful to the subscribers in general, at whose expense they had been feasted, especially to MR. ALLEN, the assistant clerk, to whose kind hearted exertions in the collection of subscriptions they were mainly indebted for their feast, and who had obtained money sufficient to give the paupers a tea on New-year's day. It has been a real, hearty, merry Christmas for the poor people; and it did one's heart good to see the happy faces of the company, and their industrious application in the business which had called them together, and to hear the merry carol which followed "the withdrawal of the cloth". The Rev's J. W. Hawksley, sen. and jun., and their ladies, and several respectable inhabitants of the neighbour-hood, attended to witness the festivities.

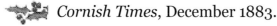 *Cornish Times*, December 1883.

Liskeard: On Christmas Eve the mayor of Liskeard (Mr

W Polkinghorne) gave a tea in the town hall to 200 poor people in the town. The volunteer band was present and rendered festive music.

 M. A. Courtney. 1890.

A very general meal for poor people in some parts of the county on Christmas eve was pilchards and unpeeled potatoes boiled together in one "crock".

 Christmas Eve at Jamaica Inn.

John Burton was the proprietor of the Old Curiosity Shop Falmouth.

JOSEPH BURTON, of Stockport, Lancashire, came, for what reason is unknown, to Cornwall in 1830, and set up a china and glass shop at Bodmin; and married at Launceston a Miss Clemo.

Old Joseph was a sturdy Radical and Nonconformist. He was a vigorous and loud supporter of the Ballot Society, the Liberation Society, and the United Kingdom Alliance. He was also a vehement and "intemperate" teetotaller. He died at Bodmin 19th July, 1876. John was one of a whole string of children, and as the "cloam" shop did not bring in a large profit, and John was one among many, he had to go into life very inefficiently equipped with education. But he had inherited from his father a masterful spirit, and had his own independent views, and it was soon a case between them of flint and steel, and sparks flew out.

John and his brother Joe were sent round the country hawking pots and glass.

"I well remember the 24th December, 1853," said John Burton. "Myself and my late brother Joe (who afterwards became a well-known auctioneer) rose at five o'clock in the morning, fed the horse, and made a start at 5.45 a.m. with a waggon-load of goods. The morning was dark, and when we came to Callywith turnpike gate it was closed. We knocked Henry Mark, the toll-keeper, up to let us through. He looked out of the window and at first refused to let us pass until daylight. We firmly told him that we would certainly unhang the gate and pass through without paying the toll. This fetched the old man down, with his long coat, knitted nightcap, with horn lantern in his hand. He opened the gate and told us, 'You Burtons ought to be poisoned for breaking a man's rest.' A lot we cared for his curses. Fairly on the road, we were as happy as sandboys. Having delivered the goods, and fairly on the way home, we stopped at the Jamaica Inn, where the old mail-coaches used to change their horses, to feed our horse, not forgetting ourselves. After giving 'Old Dapper' his feed of oats, we went into the inn kitchen, where we ordered a hot meal. The landlady asked, 'What would you like?' She suggested a hot squab pie, which she took out of a huge kitchen range well loaded with burning turf, the odour of which increased our appetites considerably. We polished off the pie and pocketed the crust to eat on the moors when homeward bound".

The Jamaica Inn is in the midst of the Bodmin Moors. In the time of the mail-coaches from London by Exeter to Falmouth it was a house of great repute. But when the trains ran, and coaches were given up, it fell from its high estate, was converted into a temperance house, was far from clean, harboured innumerable fleas, and did little business. Of late it has entirely recovered its credit. It stands nine hundred feet above the sea. There are now there at Bolventor a church and a school. A bleak, wind-swept moor all about it. Dozmare Pool, haunted by

Tregeagle, is near by—and in June the meadows around are a sheet of gold from the buttercups. But to return to John Button's reminiscences.

"When the landlady came in and saw that we had finished the pie, she looked with amazement towards us.

'Why, drat you boys, whativer have 'ee done with the pie?'

'Why, ate'n, misses. Do'y think we called the horse in to help us, or what?'

'No,' she smartly replied, 'I should 'a thawt you had the Bodmunt Murlicha (Militia) here to help 'ee out. I never seed such gluttons in my life.'

"When we asked what we had got to pay, she said, 'Sixpunce for the crist, threepunce for the suitt, ninepunce for the gibblets, and eightpunce for apples, onions, spice, currants and sugar, and fourpunce for baking 'un; two dishes ov tay, tuppunce; that'll be two-and-eightpunce altogether, boys.'

'All right, missus, here's the posh.'

"She asked us out of bravado if we could eat any more. We said, 'Yes; we could do with some Christmas cake.'

She politely told us that she shouldn't cut the Christmas cake until the next day. 'But you can have some zeedy biscays, if you like.'

'All right.' And in she brought them, which we also polished off. Afterwards she demanded fourpunce for them.

'All right, misses, the fourpunce charged for baking the pie will pay for the biscuits, so us'll cry quits,' which joke the old woman swallowed with a good laugh."

John Burton proceeds to describe the Christmas merry-making at the inn that night. Jamaica Inn had not then become a temperance hotel. The moormen and farmers came in, the great fire glowed like a furnace. The wind sobbed without, and piped in at the casement—"the souls on the wind", as it was said, the spirits of unbaptized babes wailing at the windowpane, seeing the fire within, and condemned to wander on the cold blast without.

To the red fire, and to the plentiful libations, songs were sung, among others that very favourite ballad of the "Highwayman":

I went to London both blythe and gay,
My time I squandered in dice and play,
Until my funds they fell full low,
And on the highway I was forced to go.

Then, after an account of how he robbed Lord Mansfield and Lady Golding, of Portman Square:-

I shut the door, bade all good night,
And rambled to my hearts delight.

After a career of riot and robbery, the Highwayman at length falls into the toils of Sir John Fielding, who was the first magistrate to take sharp and decisive measures against these pests of society. Then the ballad ends:-

When I am dead, borne to my grave,
A gallant funeral may I have;
Six highwaymen to carry me,
With good broadswords and sweet liberty.
Six blooming maidens to bear my pall
Give them white gloves and pink ribbons all;
And when I'm dead they'll say the truth,
I was a wild and a wicked youth.

One of the local characters who was present on that Christmas Eve was Billy Peppermint. As he was overcome with drink, the young Burtons conveyed him from the Jamaica Inn about ten miles, and then turned him out of their conveyance, and propped him up against the railings of a house in Bodmin, as he was quite unable to sustain himself.

That night the carol singers were making their round, and as they came near they piped forth: "When shepherds watched their flocks by night, all seated on the ground, an angel of the Lord appeared, and- "Whereon Billy roared forth:

"When I am dead they'll say the truth,
I was a wild and a wicked youth,"

and rolled over and fell prostrate on the ground.

CORNISH CAROLS

J. H. Matthews. *History of... St Ives*, 1887.

A funny story is told in St Ives to the effect that an elderly lady, one of the most respected inhabitants of the town, was awakened one night, about Christmas time, by a loud knocking at the street-door. She looked out of her window and asked who was there, and what they wanted. 'Mr. Jones, Esquire!' answered a voice in the darkness. 'Ah, well,' replied the lady, 'he doesn't live here, so please go away.' In a short time, however, the knocking was repeated, while a sound as of voices in concert was borne on the midnight air. Again the disturbed lady asked, 'Who are you?' and again came the vague reply, 'Mr. Jones, Esquire!' Indignantly she rejoined that Mr. Jones, Esquire, would receive the contents of her water-jug unless he quickly took himself off. She was no more disturbed, nor was it till a later day that the good lady learned that her rest had been troubled by 'Mr. Jones' choir' from the parish church, singing carols to honour the approach of Christmas.

 One & All Magazine, December 1868.

The Carol Singers

Now dawns the morn of Christmas,
And ere the laggard sun
Has time to show his crimson face,
The snowfall has begun;
The feathery flakes descend;
And on the lawn, the field, the road,
In one white carpet blend.

Come, draw the curtains tighter,
And make a merry blaze;
Light up the warm and cosy room,
And then what fun we'll raise!
We'll sing some pretty carols
In honour of the day;
And then a pleasant simple game
The boys and girls will play.

Hark! Stay those noisy gambols-
I hear a pleasant strain
Of children's music at the door-
Hark! There it is again!
They are the carol singers,
Who'll sing at our desire;
And there we'll have them in a while,
To warm them at the fire.

The snowfall now is over,
The sky begins to show,
So now I think we'd better let
Our little travelers go,
With just one other carol
In honour of this day,
Whereon the Saviour came from heaven
To take man's doom away.

William Bottrell. *Stories and Folk-lore of West Cornwall,* 1880. Music and words of the carol inserted from another source.

 Some of us remember when it was a custom, in the parishes of West Cornwall, for a few elderly persons to meet in Church, late on Christmas Eve, and sing till after midnight, a good number of cheerful, quaint old carols, which were quite different from the solemn Christmas hymns that have supplanted them.

The favourite carols, for the most part contained such legends as are preserved in the Mystery or old Miracle Plays, which continued to be performed in the western parishes, on Sunday afternoons, down to Elizabeth's reign or later. Others may have been derived from the Apocryphal Gospels.

Such, for instance, are the circumstances referred to in the Cherry-Tree carol, beginning with "Joseph was an old man, an old man was he."

The Cherry-tree Carol

Traditional: Mediaeval.

Known in Cornwall

This form of the Carol is suitable for general use.

1. When Joseph was an old man, an old man was he; He married sweet Mary of fair Galilee; And as they went a walking in the garden so free, Fair Mary spied cherries upon a tall tree.

1. When Joseph was an old man, an old man was he;
   He married sweet Mary of fair Galilee;
   And as they went a walking in the garden so free,
   Fair Mary spied cherries upon a tall tree.

2. "O get those cherries, Joseph, which there I can see,
   O get those sweet cherries and give them to me."
   But Joseph spake unkindly, and thus answer'd he:
   "I'll not pluck those cherries to give unto thee."

3. Then Mary said to Cherry-tree, "Bow down to my knee,
   That I may pluck cherries, by one, two and three."
   The highest branch, obedient, bowed down to her knee:
   "Thus may you see, Joseph, those cherries are for me."

4. As Joseph was a-walking, he heard Angels sing,
   "This night shall be born our Heavenly King.
   He shall not be born in house or hall,
   Nor in Heavenly mansion, but in an ox-stall.

5. "He shall not be clothed in purple or pall;
   But all in fair linen as wear babies all.
   He shall not be rocked in silver nor gold,
   But in a wooden cradle that rocks on the mould."

6. Then Mary took her Baby, she dress'd Him so sweet,
   She laid Him in a manger all there for to sleep.
   And as she stood o'er Him she heard Angels sing:
   "O bless our dear Saviour, our Heavenly King!"

Many other examples might be given of these legendary pieces, which are now almost forgotten.

We were delighted, however, last Christmas, to hear a few youngsters singing in Penzance streets the pleasant one called "The Sunny Bank," or "The Three Ships", which is also very old.

Among those of special interest may be noticed "In those Twelve Days," "The Joys of Mary," and "Man's Duty." Slightly different versions of these are common here and in Wales; and according to Mr. W. Sandys, there is a Breton song, as old as the fifth century, in the dialect of Cornouaille, called "Ar Rannou," or "Les Series," arranged as a dialogue between a Druid and his disciple on their ancient maxims and rites, which is similar in idea and construction to "In those Twelve Days," or "What is that which is but one."

The early missionaries engrafted on this ancient Armorican poem a Latin hymn, in the same form, where the series of twelve subjects is connected with the Christian religion and agrees with those of the carol, "What is that which is but one?"

At the end of each verse in the Druids Song, the Latin hymn, and the three last mentioned carols, all the previous

84

subjects are repeated in the style of "The House that Jack built." The whole piece can be constructed from the last verse. [That of "The Joy of Mary," is an example. G.P.]

Old country folk may still be often heard chanting this ancient effusion, with all its repetition it is more frequently, however, recited or taught to children as a kind of pious exercise for their memories at Christmastide.

Cornish people have been famous for their carols from an early date. Scawen says:- "They had them at several times, especially at Christmas, which they solemnly sung, and sometimes used in their churches, alter prayers, the burthen of them being "Novell, Novell, goad news, good nova, of the Gospel."

These old joyful Christmas songs have long held their own — thanks to their wonderfully interesting legends and their lively tunes, that seem like the echoes of merry peals of bells.

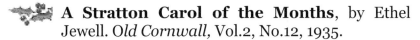 **A Stratton Carol of the Months**, by Ethel Jewell. *Old Cornwall,* Vol.2, No.12, 1935.

Stratton, in common with many other small towns in Cornwall, has a very interesting collection of Carols, but this Carol of the Months, which has recently come to light (*1931*), is as far as I can find out, unique in Cornwall, and the discovery of it is only another instance of how much and how varied is the store of folk lore still existing in our midst.

It was in 1931, that in a conversation with another Stratonian, Mrs English, of Bradford Manor, Devon, our talk drifted to some old inhabitants of Stratton, amongst them a mother and daughter, named respectively, Lizzie and Jinnie Kempthorne.

Immediately their names were mentioned, memory called up their figures and their homes. At that time they lived in a tiny two roomed cottage at Gibraltar Square, since tumbled down. The floor downstairs was of beaten earth and the interior of the cottage, even on bright days was so dim that it was no wonder that the upper latch was invariably open to give the dwelling extra air and light. Moreover I never seem to remember seeing the two women without their bonnets. To my childish imagination it appeared as if they wore them even in bed.

Mrs English then told me that Lizzie, the elder woman was for many many years a kitchen visitor for Christmas Day at St. Cyprian's the home of Mrs English's Doctor, John King, and that after dinner on Christmas evening, Lizzie would come into the drawing room and sing this old song. She would then turn around very solemnly three times and say to the assembled company. "Good evening ladies and gentlemen all, I wish you a merry Christmas and a happy New Year".

I was so interested in this story that I got Miss Grace English to give me the bare notes of the air, and this together with the words and the suggestion that perhaps the "turning around" might refer to the Trinity I sent to Dr Ralph Dunstan.

The following is part of Dr Dunstan's letter in reply.

"The Carol of the Months" is very interesting I send you what I think might be the rendering, and a simple harmony such as might be sung if there happened to be "a company of singers". "Turning about three times" might possibly in later times refer to the Trinity, but Dr Dexter the distinguished Cornish antiquarian, says it was undoubtedly the usual "turnings" in Sun-worship observance, common in every part of the world. Christmas Day was one of the chief dates of Sun-worship Festivals, the date being borrowed by the early Christians and allotted to that of the birth of Christ.

This makes the Carol in some form or other a very ancient one, and you have certainly rescued a noteworthy example of old custom." Dr Dunstan also added that he arranged a copy of the Carol, with details of its history, for insertion into the Second Part of his Cornish Song Book if and when it should ever be published. Alas! Very soon after this he died, and Cornish music lost its best exponent.

Carol of the Months

January's when cold winds do blow,
February brings us frost and snow,
March is when young lambs do play,
April brings us flowers so gay,
May is when the fields are green,
June is when new hay is seen,
July's days are very warm,
August brings the thunder storm,
September's harvest fields are clear,
October's when we brew fine beer,
November dreariest days in the year,
December ends the fleeing year.

The Dilly Song

Sabine Baring-Gould. *Songs and ballads of the West: a collection made from the mouths of the people*, 1891.

A great number of versions of this song have been taken down, and a good many were sent to the pages of the Western Morning News in 1888 from various parts of

Devon & Cornwall. This is known throughout Cornwall and is indeed still sung in the chapels.

When a party of amateurs performed some "Songs of the West" in Cornwall in 1890 the Dilly song always provoked laughter among the good folk at the back of the halls; this puzzled the performers till they enquired into the reason for the laughter and learned that people laughed because it was their familiar chapel hymn. In the text, I have given the version of the words with least of the religious element in them.

Come, and I will sing you.
What will you sing me?
I will sing you One o
What is your One o?
One of them is all alone and ever will remain so.

Come, and I will sing you.
What will you sing me?
I will sing you Two o
What is your Two o?
Two of them are lily-white babes, dressed all in green o.

Come, and I will sing you.
What will you sing me?
I will sing you Three o
What is your Three o?
Three of them are strangers, o'er the world they range o.

Come, and I will sing you.
What will you sing me?
I will sing you Four o
What is your Four o?
Four it is the Dilly hour, when blooms the gilly flower o.

THE DILLY SONG.

P & W 1506.

Come, and I will sing you.
What will you sing me?
I will sing you Five o
What is your Five o?
Five it is the Dilly Bird never seen but heard o.

Come, and I will sing you.
What will you sing me?
I will sing you Six o
What is your Six o?
Six the Ferryman in the boat that on the river floats o.

Come, and I will sing you.
What will you sing me?
I will sing you Seven o
What is your Seven o?
Seven is the crown of heaven, the shining stars be seven o.

Come, and I will sing you.
What will you sing me?
I will sing you Eight o
What is your Eight o?
Eight it is the morning break, when all the worlds awake o.

Come, and I will sing you.
What will you sing me?
I will sing you Nine o
What is your Nine o?
Nine it is the pale moonshine, the pale moonshine is nine o.

Come, and I will sing you.
What will you sing me?
I will sing you Ten o
What is your Ten o?
Ten forbids all kinds of sin, and Ten again begin o.

Here are some of the other versions.

2. In God's own son, or Christ's natures, but in a Horrabridge (Devon) version "two are strangers o'er the wide world rangers"; another "the lily white maids" not babes.

3. The strangers are probably the Three Wise Men. In a Cornish version "Three is all eternity". In another "Three is the Thrivers".

4."The Gospel Preachers", at S. Austell, "The Evangelists."

5."Five is the Ferryman in the Boat"; at Horrabridge, "The Dillybird"; another, "The Nimble Waiters".

6."The Cherubim Watchers", "The Crucifix", "The Cherry-bird Waiters". In an American version "The Ploughboys under the Bowl", "The Cheerful Waiters".

7."The Crown of Heaven", see Rev. i., 16, but more likely the Pleiades, "The Seven Stars in the Sky".

8."The Great Archangel", "The Archangels"; at Horrabridge, "Eight is the daybreak".

9."Nine are the Nine Delights", i.e., the Joys of Mary. "The Moonshine, bright and fine". "The Pale Moonshine". "The nine that so bright do shine".

10."The Commandments". "Begin again".

11."The Eleven Disciples". "They who go to Heaven".

There are very similar verses in German and Flemish. The Flemish version in Coussemaker: "*Chants populaires des Flamands*", with three variants of the air, which is a corruption of "Adeste fideles". The Scottish version in Chambers "*Popular Rhymes of Scotland*", 1842, p. 50. *Dilly,* as applied to the song, the hour, the bird, is probably the Festal Song, &c. (Welsh *dillyn*, pretty, gay, pl. *dillynion,* fineries, jewels.)

Sir Arthur Sullivan has introduced a song of the same character into his "*Yeoman of the Guard*", but the melody is not quite the same as ours.

The air to which the Dilly Song is sung in Somersetshire is similar to ours, and is, in fact, an artistic canon.

This song is very familiar throughout Brittany, as "Gousper ou Kerné", Les Vêpres de Cornouaille.

"Dis-moi ce que c'est qu'un?
Un Dieu, sans plus, qui est au ciel.
Qu'est-ce que c'est que deux?
Deux testaments.
Les trois Personnes de Ia Trinite.
Quatre Evangélistes," &c.

"*Chansons populaires de la Bretagne*", par Luzel, 1890, p.88. Also M. Villemarque gives two rude melodies (Barz-Breiz, 1846, Nos. I. & VIII.) to which it is sung by the Bretons. There was a Mediæval Latin form of the song which began "Unus est Deus". A Hebrew form as one for instructing children in truths, is printed in Mendez: "*Service for the First Night of the Passover*", London, 1862. It begins: "Who knoweth one? one is God who is over heaven and earth". The numbers go up to thirteen.

"Thirteen divine attributes, twelve tribes, eleven stars, ten commandments, nine months preceding childbirth, eight days preceding circumcision, seven days of the week, six hooks of the Mischna, five books of the law, four matrons, three patriarchs, two tables of the Covenant, but one is God alone, &c.

A Moravian form is in: Joseph Wenzig. *Westslawischer Märchenschatz*, 1857, p.295.

Inglis Gundry. Cornish Folk Songs and Carols. *Old Cornwall*, Vol.6, No.5, 1962.

In 1929 Ralph Dunstan published his "Cornish Song Book". Dunstan's aim was clearly to give Cornish people a book they could have on their pianos, ready for convivial musical occasions, such as were more common in the days before wireless became the grand arbiter of entertainment. He devoted a valuable section to Carols of the true Cornish type.

Dilly Carol (Gwennap Version)

The carol consists of twelve units, each of which are:

•An introductory sentence
•a question
•a reply.

The reply in each unit becomes longer with each verse, as the preceding verse is in all cases included. It is extended by a sentence added at the beginning as in the nursery rhyme: "This is the house that Jack built." The beginning of each verse of the reply is indicated in the music copy, and all that follows is part of that verse. Thus the first question and answer are followed by the first verse. The second question and answer are followed by the second and first verses. The third question and answer are followed by the third, second and first verses, and so on to the twelfth question and answer, after which all twelve verses are sung.

The verses may be sung in harmony, but the sentence and question are sung in unison.

94

Inglis Gundry. Cornish Folk Songs and Carols. *Old Cornwall*, Vol.6, No.5, 1962.

About the same time as Baring-Gould was collecting, Cornish musicians themselves began to become conscious of their heritage, at any rate in the way of carols. In 1889 R. H. Heath, organist at Redruth, published his "Cornish Carols"[6], composed by W. Eade, T. Broad, J. Coad, J. Stevens, A. Woolf" and himself. Some of these carols have no names attached to them and in his introduction Heath alludes to "these compositions as handed

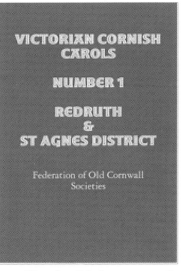

VICTORIAN CORNISH CAROLS

NUMBER 1

REDRUTH & ST AGNES DISTRICT

Federation of Old Cornwall Societies

down from father to son" and sung "in the highways and hedges" as well as "the chapels and churches". It is curious that he felt bound to apologise for these "rude compositions" and "quaint music", and he hints that he may have meddled with the harmonies in order to make them more acceptable to the prejudices of the time.

Heath's book was followed by two slim volumes called "*A selection of Old Christmas Carols and Anthems*" revised and published by T. N. Warmington, Carbis Bay, in 1912, and by "*Old Cornish Carols*" arranged by Ben Barnicoat, Polperro Press, 1927. The last mentioned is the most interesting of the three collections, "transcribed in MSS written and collected by my Grandfather, the late Francis

---

6. These have now been re-published by the Federation as *Victorian Cornish Carols*. Ed.

Woolcock, who was born in Tregoney in 1810, and died in the same place in 1888". Barnicoat refers to his Grandfather's "extensive collection of old music", which he describes as "probably copies of earlier MSS in use in the early part of the 18th century". The florid style of the music confirms that it might well come from the age of Purcell, and the free use of "consecutive fifths" suggests an even earlier origin as possible.

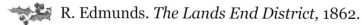 R. Edmunds. *The Lands End District,* 1862.

Throughout the Christmas week the singing of carols is very general; and early in the morning of Christmas-day, long before day-break, choirs of singers perform, oftentimes sweetly, under our windows.

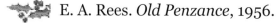 E. A. Rees. *Old Penzance,* 1956.

It was the practice of the Penzance butchers who had stalls in the old meat market to assemble outside the entrance at the close of day, on Christmas Eve, and render a fine selection of carols. Having regard to the standard of music in those days when there were no male voice choirs as at present, the singing by the Penzance butchers was very good indeed, and large crowds of people gathered around to hear them. Most of the villages in the neighbourhood could boast of excellent "Curl" parties. About 1860 the men and boys of the Mousehole Wesleyan Chapel choir always formed themselves into a carol party on the approach of Christmas. They were under the leadership of Richard Barnes who led the trebles with a violin. Mr Bond, of Newlyn, led the altos with a flute. James Harvey, the tenors with another violin, and George Barnes (father of the leader) led the basses with a bass viol. This choir left Mousehole at midnight on Christmas Eve and proceeded to Paul. After singing in the church-town they visited Trevithal, Halwyn and Reginnis in turn. At some of the houses they were invited to sing indoors, being regaled with Christmas cake and coffee; at others they were listened to from open windows.

W. D. Watson. *Old Cornwall,* Vol.3, No.7, 1940.

In conversing with an old inhabitant of Ludgvan parish at Christmas-time in 1935 on the subject of Cornish Christmas carols, he told me in connection with "Hark What mean those Heavenly Voices" a carol familiar to both of us, that when he was very young it was said that it was written "in very ancient times, soon after the Christian religion was brought to Cornwall". He had heard that on the night our Saviour was born, the Mousehole fishermen were coming home from sea, when early in the morning while they were still some miles from land a very brilliant light shone all around them and as far as their eyes could see. At the same time they heard most wonderful singing in the sky and they were all very astonished. When they came home they spread the news of these happenings, and years afterwards when the first Christian teachers came, telling the story of the Babe of Bethlehem, the fishermen were quite satisfied to accept the teaching, because they had seen and heard that some great thing had happened.

Hark! what mean those holy voices,
Sweetly sounding through the skies?
Lo! the angelic host rejoices
Heavenly hallelujahs rise.

 **Padstow Carol Singing**

John Buckingham. Padstow Old Cornwall Society.

For some Padstonians and others who are in the know, Sunday nights in December are rather special; for it is then in time honoured fashion they take to the streets of this ancient port with a set of carols unfamiliar to many other than themselves. They have been cherished and treasured for a long time now. They come from the old Carol tradition of soaring four part harmonies and we proudly call them, whatever their origins, 'The Padstow Carols'.

On the second Sunday in December the group assembled in Market Place as usual. Some had been singing in the Parish Church earlier, others have left the comfort of their homes to join the throng, some even had travelled some distance part of the growing band of regular devotees. It begins to rain. Collars are turned up and caps pulled down. Some have wisely brought umbrellas. A drop or two of rain is not going to dampen the spirits of these hardy souls.

The group forms itself into sections; Bass, Tenor, Alto and Sopranos. There are some members of organised choirs in the group but there is no membership qualification or audition process. All that is needed is a desire to be part of this strand of musical history. Most have been out already this month for the Christmas Lights Ceremony, The Buff Lodge, with St Minver Band at the British Legion and the previous Sunday "up town" where we crowd into the front room and hall of the home of Geoff and June Hicks. It seems we have been making these calls in this way for ever, but of course we know that is not true.

Roger is the leader and he announces the Carol and blows the appropriate note on his pitch pipe followed by the words 'Strike sound'. He has been singing these carols since he first came along with his Dad and proudly took over from Molly Pinch who had led the group with enthusiasm and determination for 20 years. Being over 90 was no problem to this lady. Roger remembers too his uncle Raymond and Johnny Worden fulfilling this roll.

It was in the 1960's when Johnny Worden was in charge that the words and music for all our carols were gathered together and with the help of Stephen Fuller, Inglis Gundry and others they became published by Donald Rawe's Lodenek Press as *"Strike Sound"*.

But there is singing to be done on this damp December evening. 'Rouse Rouse' is announced. Those following in the book or on song sheets find their place. The regulars stop chatting to neighbours whom they may not have seen since last year and "... isn't that Clifford home from Australia?" 'Strike Sound' and we are off, more or less all at the same time.

The voices soar into the night sky, a few onlookers have braved the elements and savour the moment. This carol we regard as truly ours. As far as we know it has not survived elsewhere.

As we might expect in carols much loved by those enthusiastic evangelical Bible Christian Methodists of the last century, there is a liberal sprinkling of Hallelujahs in this collection. 'How Beautiful upon the Mountains' so loved by our sopranos for the soaring notes they are expected to achieve, ends with a resounding 'Hallelujah! Hallelujah! Praise ye the Lord' and 'Lo he comes an Infant Stranger' from the well known Cornish Carol composer Thomas Merritt from Redruth, has them in abundance.

Here in Padstow in the past the carols were shared by all churches and today it is comforting to find Catholics, Anglicans and Methodists among the singers.

It matters not where or when this music came to us. It matters most that we have hung on to it and kept it alive. They were part of life here when the horrors of the Somme were played out, and again at the time of the threat of invasion in 1940. We sing them again with the death toll in the middle east rising daily. What has happened to "Peace on the Earth Goodwill to Men"

Thomas Merritt

Leonard H. Truran wrote the following as an introduction to his publication of *Twelve Cornish Carols*, by Thomas Merritt.

A mere forty-six years was the life-span of Thomas Merritt; who lived in an age when disease and hardships in the Cornish tin and copper mines made old men of youths, and the Biblical 'three score years and ten' was a fiction to all but the lucky few.

The son of an Illogan miner, Merritt was a natural musician who developed his musical abilities with the aid of only six months tuition before the age of eighteen. He had no patron to aid his genius; his home background was one of consistent poverty.

100

Education (at Pool Board School) ceased for him at the age of eleven, when his father died. Jobs at Carn Brea mine and Tolvaddon tin streams seemed to be destining the young Thomas to the grinding life of a mine-worker; but physical frailty and ill-health soon dictated otherwise. Before he was twenty he was beginning to earn a meagre living as a music teacher. As organist of Chili Road Chapel, and later at Fore Street Methodist Church (both at Illogan Highway, Redruth) he made his mark amongst the many dedicated musicians of the district.

By candlelight in his cottage he began to compose; and the music poured forth - oratorios, anthems, a sacred cantata, carols and hymns. Soon in the mines, on the surface and underground, his vigorous and joyful music swelled; the dark, dingy world of the underground levels, the warm, consoling atmosphere of the inns, and the fervent, religious air of the chapels, rang and resounded with his stirring compositions. When Cornish mining declined the men, migrating in masses from the Redruth area, took his tunes across the world, and today they can be heard in such far-scattered places as Grass Valley, California, the Rand, South Africa, and the Yorke Peninsula, South Australia.

Merritt was also talented as a conductor. He often directed choirs performing his own compositions. For brass and silver bands, the first love of many a Cornishman, he wrote several works, including a well-known march for the Coronation of Edward VI in 1902. Today from the barren, mine-scarred landscape of Camborne-Redruth the music of Merritt continues to swell, attracting new devotees each year.

Of all the music, however, his carols are best known and loved. They have been reprinted many times; and still the demand for them grows.

Gentle and modest Methodist that he was, Thomas Merritt attracted the attention of well-known contemporary composer Malcolm Arnold; who expressed his 'enormous admiration for a man who was able to overcome such wretched material circumstances, and give us some of the most vigorous and joyous music it has been my privilege to hear.' In 1968, on the 60th anniversary of Merritt's death, Dr. Arnold conducted a memorial concert in Truro Cathedral; massed choirs and bands gave an emotive tribute (unforgettable to those present) to the Cornish miners musicians, performing a number of his anthems and carols.

In the churchyard at Illogan can be seen a memorial in white marble, with these words on it:-

> In loving Memory of Thomas Merritt
> Who died April 17th 1908 aged 46 years.
> The languishing head is at rest,
> Its thinking and aching are o'er;
> This quiet immoveable breast
> Is heaved by affliction no more.

And on the wall of Fore Street Chapel, Illogan Highway, is a 50th anniversary plaque 'erected by Camborne-Redruth U.D.C. to commemorate with pride and gratitude the late Thomas Merritt of this parish; once organist in this chapel and composer of Christmas carols sung by Cornish men and women the world over'.

Chili Road chapel is no more; a thousand monuments of the last great mining generation are now destroyed or decaying; but the notes of Thomas Merritt's music, rising to a climax each Christmas, continue to enshrine the ancient Christian and Celtic spirit of Cornwall.

CHRISTMAS NEWS

F. Trevithick. *The Life of Richard Trevithick*, 1892.

Mr Stephen Williams of Camborne talking in 1858 about the first running of a steam powered road vehicle 1801:

"I knew Captain Dick Trevithick very well; he and I were born in the same year. I was a cooper by trade, and when Captain Dick was making his first steam-carriage I used to go every day into John Tyack's blacksmith's shop at the Weith, close by here, where they put her together.

"The castings were made down at Hayle, in Mr. Harvey's

foundry. There was a deal of trouble in getting all the things to fit together. Most of the smiths' work was made in Tyack's shop.

"In the year 1801, upon Christmas-eve, coming on evening, Captain Dick got up steam, out in the high-road, just outside the shop at the Weith. When we see'd that Captain Dick was agoing to turn on steam, we jumped up as many as could; may be seven or eight of us. 'Twas a stiffish hill going from the Weith up to Camborne Beacon, but she went off like a little bird.

"When she had gone about a quarter of a mile, there was a roughish piece of road covered with loose stones; she didn't go quite so fast, and as it was a flood of rain, and we were very squeezed together, I jumped off. She was going faster than I could walk, and went on up the hill about a quarter or half a mile farther, when they turned her and came back again to the shop. Captain Dick tried her again the next day; I was not there, but heard say that some of the castings broke. Recollect seeing pieces of the engine in the ditch years afterwards, and suppose she ran against the hedge".

 *Royal Cornwall Gazette*, 3rd January 1835.

Penzance: The weather in the neighbourhood has been for the last three weeks prior to the 26th, most delightful, more like Midsummer than Christmas. Persons were seen bathing in the bay the day before Christmas, and a species of butterfly of very elegant colour flew in at a window in the town and settled on a myrtle.

Paul: On Christmas Eve, the fishermen of Mousehole and Newlyn, lit up fifteen large candles on the pinnacles of Paul Tower, and there being no wind up they burnt as readily as if they had been in a room. These are very singular occurrences for the time of the year; but since the 26th the weather has changed and it has blown a gale from S to S.S.W. with very thick weather.

 West Briton, 21st December 1838.

Richard Oats, Innkeeper, St. Just, in Penwith, who has carried on the above business for nearly forty years past, at the "STAR INN", in that village, begs leave to return his sincere thanks to the Neighbouring Gentlemen, Commercial Gentlemen, and the Public in general, for the very liberal support he has received from them during the above period, and begs to inform them that he is about to REMOVE at Christmas next to the "COMMERCIAL INN", in the said village, which has been recently erected; with good Stabling and Lock-up Coach House, and hopes by keeping a stock of good OLD WINES, WELL-AIRED BEDS, and by strict attention to Business, to merit that share of public patronage which has hitherto been bestowed on him.

Dated Star Inn, St. Just in Penwith, Nov. 27, 1838.

 West Briton, 28th December 1838.

Christmas Souvenir

At a period when the social sympathies are most predominant, and the genial influence of "home" is felt in the highest degree – more especially by "My young misses", just arrived to spend her vacation at the "Old Hall" the most appropriate present become the first subject of consideration; a merely useful one can afford no evidence of taste, while a present possessing no claims to utility shows a want of judgment. To combine these requisites, we can hardly suggest a more fitting souvenir than Rowland's Toilet Articles, the "MACASSAR", "KALYDOR", and "ODONTO", which, from their beautifying effects on the hair, complexion, and teeth, are calculated to preserve a grateful recollection of the donor. See Advertisement.

Carharrack: In the Wesleyan chapel at this place the morning of Christmas day was solemnly ushered in by the choir of that chapel singing the beautiful piece, "Joy to the world, the Lord is come," after which prayer and singing were continued, the latter reflecting much credit on Captain RICHARD JEFFERY, the leader of the choir. In the evening an excellent discourse was delivered by the Rev. J. HARROP, from St. Luke's gospel, chap. 2nd, verse 14th, in the course of which he explained with much energy, the nature of Christ's mission. It is highly gratifying to add, that unlike past Christmas days, no Bacchanalians were seen in the public way, but many hundreds of human beings proceeding to the house of prayer.

Newlyn: On Monday, in the parish of Newlyn, Inquest on the body of THOMAS ROBERTS, aged 7 years.

The mother of deceased went to Michell to receive some Christmas charity, and locked the deceased and his sister in the house, to keep them, as she thought, out of harm's way, as the neighbours had been complaining of their being mischievous children. A neighbour, hearing screeches proceeding from the house, looked in at the window, and saw the deceased with all his clothes on fire, and his sister throwing water on him. The neighbour rendered what assistance he could, and afterwards Mr. VIGURS, surgeon, attended him; but he died in the course of the night. Verdict, "Accidental death".

West Briton, 16th December 1842.

Christmas Ball: Green Bank Hotel, Falmouth. A Ball and Supper will take place at the above Hotel, on Wednesday the 21st December instant. Stewards - Capt. ELLICE, R.N., E. HULL, Esq., Capt. FITZGERALD, John KINSMAN, Esq., Lieut. PORTER, 67th Regt. Gentlemen's Tickets 7s. 6d. Ladies ditto 5s.

 West Briton, 9th January 1846.

Christmas Provision: The week before last, the cottage labourers of Saint Stephens Coombe, in Branwell, slaughtered their twelve months old pigs against Christmas. Although the pigs, amounting to 29 in number, were not well fed, in consequence of the scarcity of potatoes, yet the whole lot together weighted 11,397 pounds, thus averaging 19 score and 13 pounds to each pit. In estimating the expense of feeding this year, it was found to be much greater than that of last year.

A Theft at Christmas: JANE ROGERS, 44, was charged with stealing 18lbs. of beef, with a quantity of rice, currants, lard, and sugar, in a linen bag and basket, the property of WILLIAM NICHOLAS, a farmer of Ludgvan. The prosecutor, on the 23rd December, had been to the Christmas market at Penzance, and bought the articles named, which he afterwards placed, for a time, for security, at the Ship and Castle, in Market-jew-street. In consequence of suspicions, the prosecutor went in pursuit of prisoner, and found her, with a woman named KITTO, driving a cart in the parish of Breage, where prisoner lived with her husband. On being questioned, the prisoner said that a neighbour of hers named RAPSON, told her to go to the kitchen of the Ship and Castle for the articles. - Guilty.

West Briton, 12th January 1849.

An Emigration Marriage: A letter from Devonport says: "A young woman, aged 22, a servant, being taken ill of typhus was removed to the workhouse at Devonport, where by attention she soon recovered. After her restoration to health she expressed a desire to emigrate to Australia if the guardians would advance the sum of £2.10s., which is necessary to be paid to the Emigration Society for outfit previous to sailing, and which money is returned them on disembarking, and the guardians having received a most satisfactory character of her from the governor of the workhouse, they agreed to do so; and she accordingly went to the office to inquire about her passage. Whilst waiting there, however, she was accosted by a respectable person, who asked her business, and if she were going to emigrate. She replied in the affirmative, when he rejoined "So am I; and if you have no objection I'll marry you previous to sailing." She replied that she was obliged for the offer, but thought it was very extraordinary and premature, seeing that he knew nothing about her; upon which he remarked that he liked her honest countenance. At length the matter was most seriously entertained, and she referred him to the service she had lately left. He at once started off to the address, and received such a satisfactory character, that on returning he immediately purchased the license, and they were married on Christmas-day. It may be added, that previous to the wedding he spent £20 for his wife's outfit, paid her passage, and returned the £2.10s. to the guardians with many thanks".

Royal Cornwall Gazette, 28th December 1865.

School Treat at Callington: Our worthy rector, Rev. L.V. Thornton and his kind hearted and generous wife, gave a very excellent tea to two hundred children – day and Sunday scholars – at their sole charge, on the 21st; and after the children had finished their tea, a most substantial meal was given to about forty of the parishioners connected with their schools. After tea, there was exhibited a beautiful Christmas Tree, which had been got up by the Misses Thornton and some other ladies, from which was distributed a very pretty present to every child, and also a more valuble and suitable memento to the teachers in the schools. The evening was finished by a magic lantern, exhibited by the rector, the astronomical part of which was very instructive, and the remainder gave infinite fun and amusement to the children.

Altogether it was a great success, and every one present must have felt a debt of gratitude to the providers. – One hundred or more were regaled at South Hill, today.

St. Mary's Truro: The decoration of this church was carried out on a very extensive scale by the ladies of the congregation. The nave, aisles, and front of the gallery were festooned with evergreens, and spiral wreaths of similar material ornamented the columns, but the zeal of the fair artistes was mainly devoted to the chancel upon which a vast amount of time must have been spent, and the effect produced shows it was a real labour of love. The pulpit and lectern are particularly deserving of notice, for the exquisite taste displayed in their ornamentation, and a very handsome shield, forming a temporary reredos, extending the width of the altar was presented by Mrs Arthur Willyams. It is of semi-circular form, with a border of everlastings and evergreens, tastefully arranged, enclosing, on a scarlet ground, a gilt cross and crown, either side of which are stars done in blue and gold. Mrs Willyams also presented two kneeling cushions as a Christmas offering.

Christmas Markets

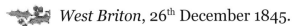 *West Briton*, 26th December 1845.

Liskeard: The Christmas show of meat at this market, on Saturday, was one of the finest ever seen. The beef produced by Mr. SNELL, of Landrake, excelled any that has been brought to this market for many years. The mutton was of a superior quality, especially that from a sheep slaughtered by Mr. ELFORD.

Launceston Castle

Launceston: This market was supplied with a finer show of meat than has been seen there in any former year.

Truro: The demand for good cheer at this season of the year, rendered the market at Truro, on Wednesday last, an extremely busy one; the crowd of people in the butter and poultry market, particularly, being excessive. In the butchers' market there was a good supply of meat, which fetched high prices - beef selling from 7d. to 7 1/2 d. per lb, and legs of mutton at 7d. Of other provisions the supply was not so large as that of last year, and consequently, higher prices were maintained. Geese fetched from 6 1/2d. to 7 1/2 d. per lb; ducks from 1s.9d. to 2s. each; butter 13d. per lb; eggs seven for 6d.; potatoes from 6d. to 9d. per gallon. These quotations will show that Sir Robert Peel's dreaded Tariff has not yet done much in the way of lowering the prices of some articles to the consumer.

Royal Cornwall Gazette, 31st December 1847.

Helston Christmas Market: A large show of all kinds of food was provided by the different purveyors who found a ready sale for their commodities. The vegetables, meat and poultry markets were abundantly supplied. The finest beef in the market was exhibited at the stalls of Messrs. Chynoweth and Bishop, who had a splendid cow, fed by Joseph Hendy Esq. of Gwills estate, in Cury, near Helston. This was acknowledged to be the best fed cow ever exhibited in Helston market and was purchased for the sum of 30 guineas.

The loss of the potato has also been a great blow to the miner. Whether a tutman or a tributer, he generally works but about eight hours a day, and has thus a great deal of spare time on hand. It is, in more respects than one, of the utmost importance that this spare time should be well employed. So long as the potatoes succeeded, the spare time of the miner was in perhaps the majority of instances, well employed. If he had not a garden attached to his house, he generally rented a piece of ground, which he applied to the production of potatoes and other vegetables. These holdings varied from an acre to two or three acres of land, and were generally leased to him for three lives. In some districts, where the land had not been cultivated before, he would have a piece of waste land and enclose it, and thus reduce it to cultivation. A great deal of the surface of Cornwall has been thus reclaimed, and a large proportion of the Lord Falmouth's present rental is derived from land originally reduced by the miner. The miner was thus always secure of a good supply of potatoes, and other vegetables for the climate of Cornwall is admirably adapted for the production of vegetables of almost all kinds. The quantity of potatoes which he produced was frequently not only sufficient for the consumption of his family, but also for the feeding of one or two pigs. When he killed his pig, which he generally did about Christmas, he would sell enough of it to enable him to buy another young pig or two, sufficient being still left to supply some animal food to his family. When he killed two pigs, which was not unusual, he would sell enough to enable him not only to buy two other young pigs for the succeeding year, but also to pay the rent for his plot of ground, so that the remainder of the pork, and the potatoes and other vegetables, which he had for the use of his family, were all so much clear profit to him. The extent to which this enhanced both his own and his family's comforts may be easily imagined.

CHRISTMAS GAMES

One & All Magazine.

Whilst searching the archives in the Morrab Library in Penzance I came across a rare bound volume of a magazine produced in Penzance in 1868. The name of the publication was "*One and All*". This has provided some of the information given below. Miss M. A. Courtney of Penzance published "*Cornish Feasts and Folklore*" in 1890. In this book she records a number of the Cornish Christmas traditions still in use in the late 19th century and others which were no longer practiced.

George Pritchard

Card Games

After candlelight many games were played around the open fires. During the twelve days of Christmas card-playing was a very favourite amusement with all classes. In her book "*Cornish Feasts and Folklore*" Miss M. A. Courtney explained a number of card and table games played in Cornish homes at Christmas.

Swabbers: Whilst the old people enjoyed their game of whist with 'swabbers', the young ones had their round games. I will append the rules of two or three for those who would like to try them. Whist (or whisk, as I have heard an old lady call it and maintain that was its proper name) with 'swabbers'. This game, which was played as recently as 1880, nightly, by four maiden ladies at Falmouth, is like ordinary whist; but each player before beginning to play puts into the pool a fixed sum for 'swabs'. The "swab-cards" are - ace and deuce of trumps, ace of hearts and knave of clubs. The four cards are of equal value; but should hearts be trumps the ace would count double [swab = a card entitling its holder to a share of the stakes].

Board-'em: A round game that can be played by any number of players, from two to eight; it is played for fish, and there must never be less than six fish in the pool. Six cards are dealt to each person; and the thirteenth, if two are playing, the nineteenth if three, and so on, is turned up for trumps. The fore-hand plays; the next player, if he has one, must follow suit, if not, he may play another suit, or trump. The highest card of the original suit, if not trumped, takes the trick and one or more fish, according to the number staked. If you have neither card in your hand that you think will make a trick you may decline to play, in which case you only lose your stake; but should you play and fail to take a trick you pay for the whole company, and are said to "be boarded".

Ranter-go-round: Formerly played in four divisions marked with chalk upon a tea-tray; or even, in some cases, on a bellows - it is now played on a table, and is called "Miss Joan". Any number of players may join in it. The first player throws down any card of any suit, and says:- "Here's a ------- as you may see. 2nd player Here's another as good as he. 3rd player And here's the best of all the three. 4th player And here's Miss Joan, come tickle me." The holder of the fourth card wins the trick. He sometimes added the words wee-wee; but these are now generally omitted. If the person sitting next to the fore-hand has neither one of the cards demanded (one of the same value as the first played, in another suit, he pays one to the pool, as must all in turn who fail to produce the right cards. The player of the third may have the fourth in his hand, in which case all the others pay. The holder of the most tricks wins the game and takes the pool.

Pinny-ninny: I once, about thirty years since, at this season of the year, joined some children at Camborne who were playing a very primitive game called by them "pinny-ninny". A basin turned upside down was placed in the centre of a not very large round table. The players were supplied with small piles of pins - not the well-made ones sold in papers, but clumsy things with wire heads - "pound pins". A large bottle full of them might, then, always be seen in the general shop window of every little country village. Each in turn dropped a pin over the side of the basin, and he whose pin fell and formed a cross on top of the heap was entitled to add them to his own pile. This went on until one player had beggared all the others. Poor children before Christmas often begged pins to play this game, and their request was always granted by the gift of two. A wishing-well, near St. Austell, was sometimes called Pennameny Well, from the custom of dropping pins into it. Pedna-a-mean is the old Cornish for "heads-and-tails".

Party Games

Shadow-Buff: This game is played as follows:- If there is a white curtain at the window it may be fastened at the bottom, so as to make a smooth surface; or in the absence of a white curtain a tablecloth may be fastened upon the wall. The one chosen to act the part of shadow-buff sits before the curtain, with their back to the light and before the company. When all is arranged they pass by on the opposite side of the room, so as to cast their shadow on the white surface. Shawls or any other articles of dress may be put on and other means used to disguise themselves, such as walking lame, &c. Buffy is to guess the name, and when correct the person named is to change places.

Copenhagen: First procure a long piece of tape

or twine sufficient to go round the whole company, who must stand in a circle, holding in each of their hands a part of the string, the last takes hold of the two ends of the tape. One remains standing in the center of the circle, who is called "the Dane", and who must endeavor to slap the hands of one of those who are holding the string before they can be withdrawn. Whoever is not sufficiently alert, and allows their hands to be slapped, must take the place of the Dane, and in their turn try to slap the hands of some one else.

The Cat and the Mouse: Let all the company join hand in hand in a circle, except one, who is placed inside, called the mouse, and another outside, called the cat. They begin by running round, raising the arms; the cat springs in at one side, and the mouse jumps out at the other; they then suddenly lower the arms so that the cat cannot escape. The cat goes round mewing, trying to get out, and as the circle must keep dancing round all the time, she must try and find a weak place to break through. As soon as she gets out she chases the mouse, who tries to save herself by getting within the circle again. For this purpose they raise their arms. If she gets in without being followed by the cat, the cat must pay a forfeit, and try again; but if the mouse is caught she must pay a forfeit. Then they name who shall succeed them, they fall into the circle, and the game goes on as before.

Thus says the Grand Mufti: This favourite game is played as follows:- One of the party stands up in a chair who is called the "Grand Mufti", who makes whatever motion he pleases, such as putting his hand to his heart, stretching out his arms, smiting his forehead, making a sorrowful face, &c. At each movement he calls

117

out, "Thus says the Grand Mufti", or, "So says the Grand Mufti". When he says, "Thus says the Grand Mufti", every one must make the same motion; but when he says, "So says the Grand Mufti", every one must keep still. A forfeit for a mistake.

Fettered Fight: This game is only fit for boys, and is played thus:- All clasp their hands under their knees, and, consequently, leave only their feet free; they arrange themselves in equal numbers in opposite lines, and try to upset their companions. When they are down it is almost impossible for them to rise, owing to their hands being under them. Their clumsy attempts to do so cause the fun of the game.

My Lady's Toilet: Each having taken the name of some article of dress, chairs are placed for all the party but one, so as to leave one chair too few. They all sit down but one, who is called the lady's maid and stands in the centre; she then calls out, "My lady's up and wants her shoes", when the one who has taken that name jumps up and calls, "Shoes", sitting down directly. If they do not rise as soon as called, they must pay a forfeit. Sometimes she says, "My lady wants her whole toilet", then every one must jump up and change chairs, and as there is a chair too few, of course it occasions a scramble, and whoever is left standing must be lady's maid, and call to the others as before.

Magic Music: While one is dismissed those remaining fix on something which he must do on his return, perhaps snuff the candles, or stir the fire. He is then called in, and another seats himself at the piano, and plays loudly or softly, as the actions of the person may seem to approach nearer or recede farther from the object

118

he is to touch. If he seems to have an idea of what is expected of him, the player directly increases the loudness of the music, but begins playing softly again as soon as he appears to have lost it. If unable to guess he must forfeit.

French Blind Man: In this game, instead of blindfolding one of the players, his hands are tied behind him, and in that difficult way he must endeavor to catch one of his a companions, who must, when caught, submit to the same restraint.

Proverbs: One of the company having left the room, the rest select some proverb in his absence, say, for instance, "Honesty is the best Policy". On his re-admittance he must ask a random question of one of the party, who in his reply must contrive to introduce the word "honesty". Thus, supposing the question, might say, "Yes, I have, and very nearly lost my purse but it was picked up by a boy, who ran after me with it, and whose 'honesty' I was very glad to reward". He then passes on to the next who must bring in "is", and so on, till the whole proverb has been mentioned. The person must then guess it, or forfeit, and those who have been unable to bring in their word must likewise forfeit. It is an extremely amusing game. from the laughable way in which some of the words are necessarily introduced.

The proverb selected should be a familiar one, and, if possible, to consist of as many words as there are persons composing the party.

Buff with the Wand: Having blindfolded one of the party, the rest take hold of each other's hands in a circle round him, he holding a stout stick. The players then skip round him once and stop. Buffy then stretches forth his wand and directs it by chance, and the person whom it touches must grasp the end presented, and call out three times in a feigned voice. If Buffy recognise him they change places, but if not he must continue blind till he makes a right guess.

Robin's Alight: A piece of stick was set on fire, and whirled rapidly in the hands of the first player, who repeated the words -- "Robin's alight, and if he go out I'll saddle your back". It was then passed on, and the person who let the spark die had to pay a forfeit. - (West Cornwall). This game in East Cornwall was known as:

Jack's Alive: Jack's alive and likely to live, If he die in my hand a pawn I'll give". In Cornwall forfeits are always called "pawns"; they are cried by the holder of them, saying - "Here's a pawn and a very pretty pawn! And what shall the owner of this pawn do?"

Lankyloo. *Old Cornwall*, Vol.1, No.4, 1926.

A rhyme, sung to an air that seems to be founded on that to which the words of "Jolly Miller" are sung in the well-known game, runs as follows :

"Oh, Lankyloo 's a very fine town,
And a very fine town is Lankyloo;
And I'm willing to bet with any of you
That all of my strokes (*or* notes) are thirty-two."
W.D.W. (Redruth).

or in another version, with "game" instead of "town":-
"O, Lankyloo 's a very fine game,
A very fine game is Lankyloo;
And I will bet with any of you
That all of my strokes are thirty-two."
J.T. (Camborne).

There can be little doubt that the word "game" is the right one, for in this version the rhyme is still associated with a game, in which the person who sings it makes strokes with a pencil on a slate, keeping time with the rhyme. If correctly made the strokes should amount to thirty-two in all.

In France similar games are played especially by schoolgirls, a piece of paper being given a pin-prick for every beat of the rhyme. Translated, one of these runs:

"Fifteen upon fifteen
Coming back to fifteen;
Will you wager fifteen
That fifteen are there?"

If time is kept there should be fifteen holes in the paper when all is said and done correctly. Another counts thirty-two just as our own "Lankyloo," but to this three of the seven lines are made up of *tra, la, la*:

"Ladies, let us count and see
How many of us there may be-
Our way of counting 's very free-
Tra, la, la, la, la, la,
Tra, la, la, la, la, la, lère,
Tra, la, la, la, la, la,
Thirty-two are they not there?"

The counting for this is more tricky than for "Lankyloo," which can easily be made, by ignoring unaccented syllables, to run in four lines of eight beats each; even this, however, requires a little practice to get right every time.

The name "Lankyloo" suggests that this rhyme was once used in actual gambling, even if for stakes no more valuable than pins, for it is a corruption of "Lanterloo" or "Lanktriloo," the name of the old card-game better known as "Loo," or "3, or 5, card Loo," which was a great gambling-game, especially in its "unlimited" form. Like many other card games it came to us from France, with its name *Lanturlu*, which is really an exclamation equal to "Fudge!" "Stuff-and-nonsense!" "Lanterloo" in English was used as a verb meaning to wager or hazard, and from this come "lanter" or "lant," used in English dialects in the same way, and "looed," meaning cheated or defeated at a game of chance. R.M.N.

Do as I Do: This is a very comical game, and creative of much merriment, its only fault being that it is apt to become rather too noisy.

All the players except one, who is called the leader, arrange the chairs in a semicircle, the leader placing his chair in the front and facing them. He begins by addressing them as follows "My master sends me to you, sir." They reply, "What to do? What to do?"

He answers, "To do as I do with *one*," and begins to pat his right knee with his right hand, a gesture which all the other players must imitate.

Still continuing to pat, he proceeds:—"My master sends me," &c.; and this time he answers, "To do as I do with two," and pats his left knee with his left hand.

Next time, he kicks with one foot, saying, "To do as I do with *three*," and afterwards kicks with both feet. Then he moves his head cautiously, and lastly gets up and sits down.

It is in his power to order the pace at which these actions are performed, but they must all be done in time with the first pats given to the right knee. When the players come to "Do as I do with *six*," very few of them are able to continue their game, being quite tired out with the exertion and the irrepressible laughter which is called forth by their absurd gestures.

The difficult part of this game is to combine the rapid getting up and sitting down again with the kicking, but in a little time the movement is learned, and becomes easy to perform, though very fatiguing to keep up, It is a capital game to play if any one complains of the cold, as all the players will feel decidedly warm before they have finished.

I don't think many people would play this very popular Victorian parlour game today.

Snip Snap Dragon: A shallow bowl filled with spirit and currants was put on a table and the spirit set alight. The players had to try and snatch the currants out of the flames and put them into their mouths.

Conundrums:

1. How many sides has a round plum pudding? - Two, inside and outside.

2. What is that when brought to table is cut but never eaten? - A pack of cards.

3. What is that that occurs once in a minute, twice in a moment and not once in a thousand years? - The letter M.

4. Why is a farmer surprised at the letter G? - Because it turns oats into Goats.

5. What makes all men and women alike? - The dark.

6. Why is coffee like an axe? - Because they both have to be ground before being used.

7. Why is an empty room like a room full of married people? - Because there is not a single person in it.

8. What is it that goes from Penzance to Saltash without moving? - The road.

THE CORNISH PLAY

A performance of the Cornish Play at St Gertrude's
Convent School, Penzance, 1957. Produced by Mrs Waller.
Back, l to r: Doctor, Wendy Boase; Turkish Knight, Yvonne Eva;
Father Christmas, Gillian Assiter; King of Egypt, Sandra Vingoe;
St George, Monica Sheehan.
Front: Dragon, Ruth Samson; Jester (Giant), Jennifer Johnston.

A pleasing account of the rendering of this old drama in a West Cornwall farm, a hundred years ago, is given by 'Uncle Jan Trenoodle' (i.e. William Sandys) in his *Specimens of Cornish Provincial Dialect.*

It was a New Year's Eve, the writer tells us, and a goodly party of friends and neighbours was gathered to spend the day at 'Cousin Nic Carnoweth's'. After a dinner consisting of 'broth, a couple of nice pluffy young mabyers (pullets), a starry-gazy (pilchard) pie, a thumping figgy-pudding, and plenty of strong drink to keep out the cold', the company seated themselves round the Christmas stock blazing cheerfully on the open hearth. Towards 'teening time', or the fall of dusk, 'there came a grinning gaukum who told us as how the guise dancers were to the door, with the ancient play of St George. Gladly did we give them leave to enter, so in they came. There was old Feyther Chrestmas with a make-wise face possed (stuck) up on top of his own, and his long white wig, trapesing about and getting in his tantrums; and there was the Doctor, as they called 'un, with a three-cornered piked hat and his face all rudded and whited, with spurticles (spectacles) on top of his nawse. And there was one in a maiden's bed-gound and coats with ribands, and a nackin (handkerchief) in his hand and a gowk (sun bonnet) on his head. Other youngsters were in white, with ribands tied all over their shirt sleeves, and with nackins and swords, and such caps as I never seed before. They was half a fathom high, made of pastyboord (cardboard), weth powers (heaps) of beads and loakinglass, and shreds of ould cloth stringed 'pon slivers (strips) of pith—and they strutted about so brave as lubber cocks (turkey cocks). And then they gave the word to begin, and ould 'Feyther Chrestmas' stepped out and said:

> 'Here comes I, ould Feyther Chrestmas,
> Welcome or welcome not,
> I do hope ould Feyther Chrestmas
> Will never be forgot'.

Father Christmas, having introduced the play, steps back into the half-circle of the performers, leaving the stage open for the Turkish knight. The latter struts forth in an arrogant fashion, proclaiming his superiority to any Christian knight, until, of a sudden, St George himself appears. He also is confident of his prowess, and in consequence a fight takes place in which the Turkish knight is knocked down for dead. Here the play seems like to have ended but for the timely intervention of the Doctor who, after a good deal of humorous 'gag', cures him of his 'deep and deadly wound'. Once more the Turkish knight arises to do battle, but he is speedily laid low by St George, and this time slain for good. Then in comes the Dragon, a 'fearsome-looking beast' with long teeth and scurvy jaw'. His part was not played without danger, since he was required to breathe forth sulphurous flames, an effect which was achieved by putting a lighted squib in his 'snout'. An incautious elevation of the latter by throwing the explosive compound inward might, and not infrequently did, cause severe injury to the player. After a fitting display of his fearsome qualities, the Dragon also is slain by St George who, as a somewhat unexpected reward for his valour, is given the hand of 'Sabra, the King of Egypt's daughter', in marriage.

I. G. Frazer. *Golden Bough*, 1890.

Versions of this ancient mummer's play are very numerous, and include such ill-assorted characters as 'Old Beelzebub', 'Oliver Cromwell', 'Little Man Jack', besides other comic 'supers' who were introduced by the players at will. The chief characters in the play, however, are the same in all versions, whilst the essential action hinges upon the fight between the Turkish knight and St George, the slaying of the former, his resurrection by the (now) 'comic' Doctor, and the final overthrow of both the Turkish knight and the Dragon, which concludes the play. The real interest of these homely dramas, therefore, lies not so much in their treatment of the subject, which was crude enough, but in the tracing of their long descent. By symbolizing, as in its origin it is thought to have done, the defeat of Winter through the reviving miracle of Spring, Such battles, with the more or less conscious intention of assisting the sun to regain its ascendancy after the turning point of the year, were once staged in many parts of Europe.

A. K. Hamilton Jenkin. *Cornwall and its People*, 1945.

Although many years have elapsed since the 'St George' play ceased to be a regular feature of this midwinter carnival, it was not wholly forgotten. In 1866 the Rev. W. S. Lach-Szyrma witnessed its performance by the miners of Pensilva, near Liskeard. In 1890 the villagers of Manaccan and St Martin-in-Meneage toured the play through their neighbourhood with great success. Another excellent rendering of the play was given by the boys of the Roskear School, at Camborne, during the Christmas of 1914. The intention, however, of making it an annual event was frustrated by the staff alterations caused by the war.

The writer himself when living as a child in Redruth regularly took part in 'private' performances of the 'St George' play. The version used came from Stithians, and may be found in *Old Cornwall*, Vol.1, No.1, pages 29–30. This, I think, must have differed from the 'Jack-o'-the-Green' play which Mr Miners informs me was acted at Stithians as recently as the early years of the war, and which was only discontinued there by reason of the younger men being called away to active service.

A Redruth Christmas Play. *Old Cornwall*, Vol.1, No.1, 1925. Communicated by Miss L.Eddy to Mr. A. K. Hamilton Jenkin, a witness of its performance.

Enter Jack.

Jack. I open the door, I enter in;
I hope the game will soon begin.
I'll stir up the fire and make a light,
And in this house will be a fight.

Enter King George.

King George. Here comes I, King George;
King George is my name.
With the sword and thistle by my side,
I'm sure to win the game.

Jack. You, sir?

K.G. I, sir!

Jack. Take the sword, and try, sir!

[*They fight; Jack falls.*

K.G. Now I've knocked him to the ground,
There's not a doctor to be found.
How much for a doctor?

[*A Dutch auction for a doctor takes place here. A player, perhaps the Doctor himself, leaving out the obvious 'Fifty pound,' that would complete King George's last line, calls successively. 'Forty?—Thirty? Twenty?' to each of which King George answers, 'No!' and then, 'Ten?' to which he replies, 'Bring him in'.*

Enter Doctor.

Doctor. Here comes I, old Doctor Brown;
The best old doctor in the town.

K.G. Why became you the best old doctor?.

128

Dr. By my travels.

K.G. Where did you travel?

Dr. England, Ireland, Scotland and Wales, and back to old England again.

K.G. Cure Jack!

Dr. Here, Jack, take my medicine and rise.

[*He doctors Jack, who rises; all stand back.*

Enter Jacky Sweep.

Jacky Sweep. Here comes I, old Jacky Sweep;
All the money I catch, I keep. [*sings—*
Lord Nelson, Lord Nelson, Lord Nelson I see;
with a bunch of blue ribbons tied up to his knee.

[*Here the party sings a wassail song.*

All. Whe'er it's silver or copper, I do not refuse;
Put your hand in your pocket and give what you please.
For our warsale, warsale,
And jolly come to our jolly warsale.

If the missus is sleeping, I hope she will wake,
And go to the cupboard and cut up some cake,
For our . . .

There's the missus and master sitting down by the fire,
And we poor warsale boys are travelling a mile,
With our . . .

If the missus and master don't take amiss,
And send out their daughter to give us a kiss,
With our . . .

The roads are so dirty ; our shoes are so thin
Oh, do give us something for singing so well
With our . . .

Finis.

Note. This version of the Christmas Play, performed at Redruth within the last fifteen years, is remarkable as being far closer to versions from the North of England than to other West-Country versions. Thus "Jack's" opening speech is found in Derbyshire, "Doctor Brown" is a Northern name for this important character, "Jacky Sweep" uses lines given to "Devil Doubt" in Yorkshire, and Lord Nelson is a character in Northern "Pace Egg" plays, performed at Easter. The play, though very much cut down, keeps all the essentials:—A fight; a man slain and revived by the doctor, and comic relief to the tragedy in the "Jacky Sweep", with blackened face and broom. There are several curious substitutions, as—"sword and thistle," for "sword and buckler," "Scotland and Wales," for "France and Spain," and in the Wassail Song "give what you please," instead of "choose", and "Oh do give us something for singing so well" where one expects "We've got a little pocket to put a penny in".

R. M. Nance. St. Ives 1925.

A Guise-Dance Play, St. Keverne. *Old Cornwall*, Vol.1, No.1, 1925. Communicated by Capt. F. J. Roskruge, R.N., and written after Mr. Wm. Mitchell's memory of performances over seventy years ago (c1855).

Enter Father Christmas.

Father Christmas.

Here comes I, old Father Christmas
Welcome or welcome not;
I hope old Father Christmas
Will never be forgot.
I've not come to laugh nor jeer,
But I've come to taste your beer;
And if by chance your beer is done,
I'll have some Christmas cake or bun.

He raps his stick on the ground, saying—
Come on, my children, come on!

Enter Turkish Knight.

Turkish Knight.

Here comes I, the Turkish Knight,
Come from Turkish lands to fight;
First I fought in Ireland, then I fought in Spain,
Now I've come to England's land, to fight King George
again.

Enter King George.

King George. Here comes I, King George,
A man with courage bold;
If your blood is hot,
I soon will make it cold.

*[King George and Turkish Knight fight with swords, one
falls.*

F.C. Is there a doctor to be found,
To cure this deep and deathly wound ?

Enter Doctor.

Doctor. Yes, there is a doctor to be found,

To cure this deep and deathly wound.

[*He steps forward, saying*—

I've got a little box in the west side of my breeches,
That goes by the name of Elecampane;
Drop a little on this poor man's lips,
And that will bring him to life again.

F.C. What can you cure?

Dr. The hesick, pesick, pox and gout,
If there are ninety-nine devils in,
I can drive them out.

Enter Little Man Jack, grotesquely dressed and carrying on his back the effigy of a woman.

Little Man Jack. Here comes I, Little Man Jack,

Carrying my wife upon my back. . .

[*He throws his "wife" to the ground, and all sing and dance until offered food, drink, or money.*

Finis

Note.—This is a very cut-down version of a West-country form of the Christmas Play. St. George again becomes "*King* George", but the Turkish Knight keeps his true name. There is some confusion in "Doctor's" part. He should have been asked, "What can you cure?" and have given his response (usually "If there are *nineteen* devils in, I can drive *twenty* out") before showing the little bottle, "in the *waistband* of my breeches", and curing the slain man, which important detail is not here given. "Little Man Jack", too, has lost the family of dolls that should have accompanied his wife, and his lines have been forgotten. Both of these plays are quite characteristic of the versions that are found here and there all over the country, and like every other version, however fragmentary, they are useful in piecing together the original lines of the various complete versions. We should be very glad of other Cornish unprinted versions from those whose memories are stirred by the reading of these.

R. M. Nance. St Ives 1925.

132

THE WASSAIL

 Chambers' *Book of Days,* 1863.

Another ancient custom of this season which, unlike the burning of the Christmas stock, is not yet wholly obsolete was Wassailing. This practice, which was formerly observed throughout England generally, is thus described by Chambers.

'The head of the house', he writes, 'would assemble his family around a bowl of spiced ale, from which he drank their healths, then passed it to the rest that they might drink too. The word that passed among them was the ancient Saxon phrase, 'Was ha?', that is, "to your health". Hence this came to be the wassail or wassel bowl. The poorer class of people carried round the neighbourhood a bowl adorned with ribbons, begging for something wherewith to obtain the means of filling it that they, too, might enjoy wassail as well as the rich."

On New Year's-eve in the villages of East Cornwall, soon after dusk, parties of men, from four to six in a party, carrying a small bowl in their hands, went from house to house begging money to make a feast. They opened the doors without knocking, called out 'Warsail', and sang:- "These poor jolly Warsail boys Come travelling through the mire". This custom was common one hundred and fifty years ago, and is still observed in other South-West Counties.

In Cornwall the bowl, generally made of wood, was decorated and looped around with furze blossom, flowers, ivy, and ribbons. Armed with this magnificent trophy, the wassailers visited the neighbouring farms and houses of the gentry, before whose doors they struck up the following song:

1. Now Christmas is comin'
And New Year begin.
Pray open your doors
And let us come in.

Chorus:

With our wassail, wassail,
Wassail, wassail,
And joy come with our jolly
wassail.

2. O Master and Mistress
Sitting down by the fire
While we poor wassail boys
Are traveling the mire.

Chorus:

With our wassail, wassail,
Wassail, wassail,
And joy come with our jolly
wassail.

3. This ancient house
We will kindly salute.
It is an old custom
You need not dispute.
Chorus:

4. We are here in this place,
Orderly we stand,
We're the jolly wassail boys
With a bowl in our hands.
Chorus:

Now Christ-mas is com-en and New Year be - gin, Pray o - pen your door___ and

let us come in. With our___ was - sail, was - sail, was - sail, and Joy___ come to___ our

jol - ly was - sail!

5. We hope that your apple trees
Will prosper and bear
And bring forth good cider
When we come next year.

Chorus:

7. Good Mistress and Master,
How can you forbear?
Come fill up our bowl
With cider or beer.

Chorus:

9. I wish you a blessing
And a long time to live
Since you've been so free
And willing to give.

Chorus:

6. We hope that your barley
Will prosper and grow
That you may have plenty
And some to bestow.

Chorus:

8. Good Mistress and Master,
Sitting down at your ease,
Put your hands in your pockets
And give what you please.

Chorus:

 A. K. Hamilton Jenkin. *Cornwall and its People,* 1934.

In one or two places in the West Country the wassailers still visit the orchards, sprinkling the trees with cider, to ensure their bearing plentifully in the coming year. Formerly guns were fired off at such times, in order to scare away malign spirits. At the conclusion of the ceremony, as the song suggests, the wassailers were assured of a warm welcome, which generally took the form of a glass of 'shenagrum' and a slice of the Christmas cake. The latter is still a regular feature of the Christmastide in Cornwall, and there will hardly be found a cottage, however poor, which does not attempt to provide something of the sort at this season for the entertainment of chance visitors.

The following is an account by an anonymous writer of a Christmas custom in East Cornwall:

In some places the parishioners walk in procession, visiting the principal orchards in the parish. In each orchard one tree is selected, as the representative of the rest; this is saluted with a certain form of words, which have in them the form of an incantation. They then sprinkle the tree with cider, or dash a bowl of cider against it, to ensure its bearing plentifully the ensuing year. In other places the farmers and their servants only assemble on the occasion, and after immersing apples in cider hang them on the apple-trees. They then sprinkle the trees with cider; and after uttering a formal incantation, they dance round it (or rather round them), and return to the farmhouse to conclude these solemn rites with copious draughts of cider.

Cornish folklore – Christmas Eve, by Thomas Quiller Couch, September 1883, *Western Antiquary*. The following was related to the author by an old farmer on Bodmin Moor.

In Warleggan, on Christmas-eve, it was customary for some of the household to put in the fire (bank it up), and the rest to take a jar of cider, a bottle, and a gun to the orchard, and put a small bough into the bottle. Then they said:- 'Here's to thee, old apple-tree! Hats full, packs full, great bushel-bags full! Hurrah!' and fire off the gun.

Mrs. Damant, Cowes, through Folk-Lore Society.

The words chanted in East Cornwall were - "Health to

thee, good apple-tree, Pocket-fulls, hat-fulls, peck-fulls, bushel-bag fulls". An old proverb about these trees runs as follows:- "Blossom in March, for fruit you may search, Blossom in April, eat you will, Blossom in May, eat night and day". "At one time small sugared cakes were laid on the branches. This curious custom has been supposed to be a propitiation of some spirit".

 The custom of the wassail bowl was not merely one that was experienced when someone came to your door. Washington Irving (1783-1859) whose mother was Cornish[7] gave this description in his sketch of an English "Christmas Dinner".

When the cloth was removed, the butler brought in a huge silver vessel of rare and curious workmanship, which he placed before the squire. Its appearance was hailed with acclamation; being the Wassail Bowl, so renowned in Christmas festivity. The contents had been prepared by the squire himself; for it was a beverage in the skilful mixture of which he particularly prided himself: alleging that it was too abstruse and complex for the comprehension of an ordinary servant. It was a potation,

---

7   William Irven (Irving) married Sarah Saunders 18th May 1761. Falmouth, Parish Records.

indeed, that might well make the heart of a toper leap within him; being composed of the richest and raciest wines, highly spiced and sweetened, with roasted apples bobbing about the surface.

The Wassail Bowl was sometimes composed of ale instead of wine; with nutmeg, sugar, toast, ginger, and roasted crabs; in this way the nut-brown beverage is still prepared in some old families, and round the hearths of substantial farmers at Christmas. It is also called Lamb's Wool, and is celebrated by Herrick in his [poem] "Twelfth Night".

CHRISTMAS GHOST STORIES

The Piskies in the Cellar. Robert Hunt. *Popular Romances of the West of England,* 3rd ed. 1881.

On the Thursday immediately preceding Christmas-tide (year not recorded), were assembled at "The Rising Sun" the captain and men of a stream work in the Couse below. This Couse was a flat, alluvial moor, broken by gigantic mole-hills, the work of many a generation of tinners. One was half inclined, on looking at the turmoiled ground, to believe with them that the tin grew in successive crops, for, after years of turning and searching, there was still enough left to give the landlord his dole, and to furnish wages to some dozen streamers. This night was a festival observed in honour of one Picrous, and intended to celebrate the discovery of tin on this day by a man of that name. The feast is still kept, though the observance has dwindled to a supper and its attendant merrymaking.

Our story has especially to do with the adventures of one of the party, John Sturtridge, who, well primed with ale, started on his homeward way for Luxulyan Church-town. John had got as far as Tregarden Down without any mishap worth recording, when, alas, he happened upon a party of the little people, who were at their sports in the shelter of a huge granite boulder. Assailed by shouts of derisive laughter, he hastened on frightened and bewildered, but the Down, well known from early experience, became like ground untrodden, and after long trial no gate or stile was to be found. He was getting vexed, as well as puzzled, when a chorus of tiny voices shouted, "Ho! and away for Par Beach!" John repeated the shout, and was in an instant caught up, and in a twinkling found himself on the sands of Par. A brief dance, and the cry was

140

given, "Ho! and away for Squire Tremain's cellar!" A repetition of the Piskie cry found John with his elfish companions in the cellars at Heligan, where was beer and wine galore. It need not be said that he availed himself of his opportunities. The mixture of all the good liquors so affected him that, alas, he forgot in time to catch up the next cry of "Ho! and away for Par Beach!" In the morning John was found by the butler, groping and tumbling among butts and barrels, very much muddled with the squire's good drink. His strange story, very incoherently told, was not credited by the squire, who committed him to jail for the burglary, and in due time he was convicted and sentenced to death.

The morning of his execution arrived; a large crowd had assembled, and John was standing under the gallows-tree, when a commotion was observed in the crowd, and a little lady of commanding manner made her way through the opening throng to the scaffold. In a shrill, sweet voice, which John recognised, she cried, "Ho! and *away* for France!" Which being replied to, he was rapt from the officers of justice, leaving them and the multitude mute with wonder and disappointment

Notes.

1. A "stream work" is a place where tin is obtained from the drift deposits "Streamers" are the tinners who wash out the tin.

2. Picrous day is still kept up in Luxulyan.

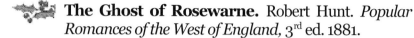 **The Ghost of Rosewarne.** Robert Hunt. *Popular Romances of the West of England,* 3rd ed. 1881.

EZEKIEL GROSSE, gent., attorney-at-law, bought the lands of Rosewarne from one of the De Rosewarnes, who had become involved in difficulties, by endeavouring, without sufficient means, to support the dignity of his family. There is reason for believing that Ezekiel was the legal adviser of this unfortunate Rosewarne, and that he was not over-honest in his transactions with his client. However this may be, Ezekiel Grosse had scarcely made Rosewarne his dwelling-place, before he was alarmed by noises, at first of an unearthly character, and subsequently, one very dark night, by the appearance of the ghost himself in the form of a worn and aged man. The first appearance was in the park, but he subsequently repeated his visits in the house, but always after dark. Ezekiel Grosse was not a man to be terrified at trifles, and for some time he paid but slight attention to his nocturnal visitor. Howbeit, the repetition of visits, and certain mysterious indications on the part of the spectre, became annoying to Ezekiel. One night, when seated in his office examining some deeds, and being rather irritable, having lost an important suit, his visitor approached him, making some strange indications which the lawyer could not understand. Ezekiel suddenly exclaimed, "In the name of God, what wantest thou?"

"To show thee, Ezekiel Grosse, where the gold for which thou longest lies buried".

No one ever lived upon whom the greed of gold was stronger than on Ezekiel, yet he hesitated now that his spectral friend had spoken so plainly, and trembled in every limb as the ghost slowly delivered himself in sepulchral tones of this telling speech.

The lawyer looked fixedly on the spectre, but he dared not utter a word. He longed to obtain possession of the secret, yet he feared to ask him where he was to find this treasure. The spectre looked as fixedly at the poor trembling lawyer, as if enjoying the sight of his terror. At length, lifting his finger, he beckoned Ezekiel to follow him, turning at the same time to leave the room. Ezekiel was glued to his seat; he could not exert strength enough to move, although he desired to do so.

"Come!" said the ghost, in a hollow voice. The lawyer was powerless to come.

"Gold!" exclaimed the old man, in a whining tone, though in a louder key.

"Where?" gasped Ezekiel.

"Follow me, and I will show thee," said the ghost. Ezekiel endeavoured to rise, but it was in vain.

"I command thee, come!" almost shrieked the ghost. Ezekiel felt that he was compelled to follow his friend; and by some supernatural power rather than his own, he followed the spectre out of the room, and through the hall, into the park.

They passed onward through the night—the ghost gliding before the lawyer, and guiding him by a peculiar phosphorescent light, which appeared to glow from every part of the form, until they arrived at a little dell, and had reached a small cairn formed of granite boulders. By this the spectre rested; and when Ezekiel had approached it, and was standing on the other side of the cairn, still trembling, the aged man, looking fixedly in his face, said, in low tones -

"Ezekiel Grosse, thou longest for gold, as I did. I won the glittering prize, but I could not enjoy it. Heaps of treasure are buried beneath those stones; it is thine, if thou diggest for it. Win the gold, Ezekiel. Glitter with the wicked ones of the world and when thou art the most joyous, I will look in upon thy happiness". The ghost then disappeared, and as soon as Grosse could recover himself from the extreme trepidation,—the result of mixed feelings,—he looked about him, and finding himself alone, he exclaimed, "Ghost or devil, I will soon prove whether or not thou liest!" Ezekiel is said to have heard a laugh, echoing between the hills, as he said those words.

The lawyer noted well the spot; returned to his house; pondered on all the circumstances of his case; and eventually resolved to seize the earliest opportunity, when he might do so unobserved, of removing the stones, and examining the ground beneath them.

A few nights after this, Ezekiel went to the little cairn, and by the aid of a crowbar, he soon overturned the stones, and laid the ground bare. He then commenced digging, and had not proceeded far when his spade struck against some other metal. He carefully cleared away the earth, and he then felt—for he could not see, having no light with him—that he had uncovered a metallic urn of some kind. He found it quite impossible to lift it, and he was therefore compelled to cover it up again, and to replace the stones sufficiently to hide it from the observation of any chance wanderer.

The next night Ezekiel found that this urn, which was of bronze, contained gold coins of a very ancient date. He loaded himself with his treasure, and returned home. From time to time, at night, as Ezekiel found he could do so without exciting the suspicions of his servants, he visited the urn, and thus by degrees removed all the treasure to Rosewarne house. There was nothing in the series of circumstances which had surrounded Ezekiel which he could less understand than the fact that the ghost of the old man had left off troubling him from the moment when he had disclosed to him the hiding-place of this treasure.

The neighbouring gentry could not but observe the rapid improvements which Ezekiel Grosse made in his mansion, his grounds, in his personal appearance, and indeed in everything by which he was surrounded. In a short time he abandoned the law, and led in every respect the life of a country gentleman. He ostentatiously paraded his power to procure all earthly enjoyments, and, in spite of his notoriously bad character, he succeeded in drawing many of the landed proprietors around him.

Things went well with Ezekiel. The man who could in those days visit London in his own carriage and four was not without a large circle of flatterers. The lawyer who had struggled hard, in the outset of life, to secure wealth, and who did not always employ the most honest means for doing so, now found himself the centre of a circle to whom he could preach honesty, and receive from them expressions of the admiration in which the world holds the possessor of gold. His old tricks were forgotten, and he was put in places of honour. This state of things continued for some time; indeed, Grosse's entertainments became more and more splendid, and his revels more and more seductive to those he admitted to share them with him. The Lord of Rosewarne was the Lord of the West. To him every one bowed the knee: he walked the Earth as the proud possessor of a large share of the planet.

It was Christmas eve, and a large gathering there was at Rosewarne. In the hall the ladies and gentlemen were in the full enjoyment of the dance, and in the kitchen all the tenantry and the servants were emulating their superiors.

Everything went joyously; and when mirth was in full swing, and Ezekiel felt to the full the influence of wealth, it appeared as if in one moment the chill of death had fallen over every one. The dancers paused, and looked one at another, each one struck with the other's paleness; and there, in the middle of the hall, every one saw a strange old man looking angrily, but in silence, at Ezekiel Grosse, who was fixed in terror, blank as a statue.

No one had seen this old man enter the hall, yet there he was in the midst of them. It was but for a minute, and he was gone. Ezekiel, as if a frozen torrent of water had thawed in an instant, roared with impetuous laughter.

"What do you think of that for a Christmas play? There was an old Father Christmas for you! Ha! Ha! Ha! Ha! How frightened you all look! Butler, order the men to hand round the spiced wines! On with the dancing, my friends! It was only a trick, ay, and a clever one, which I have put upon you. On with your dancing, my friends!"

Notwithstanding his boisterous attempts to restore the spirit of the evening, Ezekiel could not succeed. There was an influence stronger than any which he could command; and one by one, framing sundry excuses, his guests took their departure, every one of them satisfied that all was not right at Rosewarne.

From that Christmas eve Grosse was a changed man. He tried to be his former self; but it was in vain. Again and again he called his gay companions around him; but at every feast there appeared one more than was desired. An aged man - weird beyond measure - took his place at the table in the middle of the feast; and although he spoke not, he exerted a miraculous power over all. No one dared to move; no one ventured to speak. Occasionally Ezekiel assumed an appearance of courage, which he felt not; rallied his guests, and made sundry excuses for the presence of his aged friend, whom he represented as having a mental infirmity, as being deaf and dumb. On all such occasions the old man rose from the table, and looking at the host, laughed a demoniac laugh of joy, and departed as quietly as he came.

The natural consequence of this was that Ezekiel Grosse's friends fell away from him, and he became a lonely man, amidst his vast possessions—his only companion being his faithful clerk, John Call.

The persecuting presence of the spectre became more and more constant; and wherever the poor lawyer went, there was the aged man at his side. From being one of the finest men in the county, he became a miserably attenuated and bowed old man. Misery was stamped on every feature— terror was indicated in every movement. At length he appears to have besought his ghostly attendant to free him of his presence. It was long before the ghost would listen to any terms; but when Ezekiel at length agreed to surrender the whole of his wealth to any one whom the spectre might indicate, he obtained a promise that upon this being carried out, in a perfectly legal manner, in favour of John Call, that he should no longer be haunted.

This was, after numerous struggles on the part of Ezekiel to retain his property, or at least some portion of it, legally settled, and John Call became possessor of Rosewarne and the adjoining lands. Grosse was then informed that this evil spirit was one of the ancestors of the Rosewarnes, from whom by his fraudulent dealings he obtained the place, and that he was allowed to visit the earth again for

147

the purpose of inflicting the most condign punishment on the avaricious lawyer. His avarice had been gratified, his pride had been pampered to the highest; and then he was made a pitiful spectacle, at whom all men pointed, and no one pitied. He lived on in misery, but it was for a short time. He was found dead : and the country people ever said that his death was a violent one; they spoke of marks on his body, and some even asserted that the spectre of De Rosewarne was seen rejoicing amidst a crowd of devils, as they bore the spirit of Ezekiel over Carn Brea.

 William Bottrell. *Stories and folklore of Cornwall*, 1880.

As a footnote to a story concerning one Betty Toddy, and "a poor half-witted fellow called Bucca" the author comments:

This old Cornish word Bucca (still in common use) has various significations, and none very clearly defined. ...It is often applied to a poor , half-witted person of mischievious dsiposition - one about whome there is anything wierd or wisht - to a ghost, or any kind of frightful apparition, and by association of ideas to a scraecrow. By Buccaboo, which is probably a corruption of Buccadhu (black spirit) we mean Old Nick, or one of his near relations. As an example of this, there is a story told of an old lady who lived long ago at Rafta, in St. Levan. The old dame, when more than fourscore, was so fond of card playing that she would walk - almost every Winter's night, in spite of wind or weather, to the village of Trebear, distant a mile or more, that she might enjoy her favourite pastime with a family of congenial tastes who resided there. The old lady's step-daughter wished to put a stop to what she regarded as rather scandalous vagaries, the old dame seldom arriving home before the small hours of the morning; with this intention the young mistress persuaded the serving-man to array himself in a white sheet, &c., so as to personate a ghost that was accused of wandering about a lonely spot over which old madam would have to pass. The Winter's night was dark and rainy, when,m at about midnight, the ghost seated himself on the near side of Goon-proynter stile, where he had to wait two or three hours. The dear old lady passed Padz-jigga, mounted the stile, and seated herself to draw breath opposite the ghost. Over a while, she said, "Hallo! Bucca gwidden (white spirit) what cheer? And what in the world dost thee do here with Bucca Dhu close behind thee?" This cool address so frightened Bucca-gwidden that he ran off as fast as he could lay feet to ground, the old lady scampering after, clapping her hands and calling, "Good boy, Bucca-dhu; now thee west catch Bucca-gwidden and take'n away with thee!" The ghost was so frightened that he fell in a fit and was never rigt in the head after. Then he was a real bucca in the sense of our Betty's sweetheart, and the strong minded sociable old lady enjoyed many more years of her favourite pastime with her friends in Trebear.

POEMS FOR CHRISTMAS

For the Postwoman at Christmas *or* **[Poor Jenny Post],** by Francis Hingston. From: Richard Polwhele. *Biographical sketches of Cornwall,* 1831.

Ladies and gentlemen, your faithful drudge
Poor *Jenny Post*, who daily through the town,
In every sort of weather's forced to trudge,
Oft times in dripping cloak and draggled gown,
And shivering feet, plash, plashing in her shoes,
Trotting about with letters and with news.

Now at this gladsome season, when your houses
Are gay with ever greens and song and mirth -
Mince pies and eggy-flip - and gay carouses
Are ringing joyously round every hearth,
Comes Jenny Post to share your jovial cheer -
A merry Christmas and a bright new year!

Consider how you long, from day to day,
To hear her welcome foot, when on the seas
Your friends or lovers wander far away,
Braving alike "the battle and the breeze"-
Consider how you long to hear the rattle
Of Jenny Post's old pattens, pittle pattle!

And now when all the storms are hush'd and quiet
Or only at a pleasant distance grumble,
And Jenny Post would gladly mend her diet,
For Christmas-time, she thinks, by far too humble,
Dip in your well-fill'd pockets, not unwilling,
And pull her out a sixpence or a shilling.

Alas, she is a widow - and alas!
Of that unhappy sort they call bewitch'd;
She knows no reason why it came to pass:

But he - the rogue to whom her fate was hitch'd ,
Took to his heels when scarcely out of church,
And left poor Jenny Deyson in the lurch!

Else had she been a pillar not a Post -
Standing, in fair array, among the people,
Who, in their saintly meekness, rightly boast
A pious horror of the church and steeple,
And carefully make clean from stain and spatter
The outside of the cup and eke the platter.

But now, instead of resting on the shelf
Of worldly comfort and religious ease,
She is oblig'd to struggle for herself;
And, therefore, Christian neighbours! if you please
To hear and heed her annual petition,
'Twill mend at least her bodily condition!

Then give her plentifully cake and wine -
If mull'd - in frosty weather, 'tis the better;
And kindly bid her come again and dine,
If she should chance to bring a pleasant letter -
And overwhelm her with your Christmas boxes,
From Dr. Boase's down to Mr. Fox's!

Christmas Carol, composed by Atty White, the Cryer of Truro, by John Wolcot, 1738-1839.

From: R. Polwhele. *Traditions and Recollections,* 1826.

Rejoice and be merry, good folks of our town,
Since our Member and Richard Curgenwyn's come down;
As they travell'd, their dialogues, nine out of ten,
Were of nothing but princes and parliament men.

Chorus:
Then rejoice, for such tidings I never did tell,
Ever since that I've travell'd about with my bell.

Many times in his coach the great man, with an air, Took
off his own speeches to make Richard stare;
So that often Dick's locks were with terror uncurl'd, To
think he sat next the first man in the world.
Then rejoice, &c. &c.

Not like Jehu he drove, but all snugly and quiet,
For fear his arrival might kick up a riot
For fear we might tear from the traces his blacks,
And carry the coach and himself on our backs.
Then rejoice, &c. &c.

Though born so far west, he's a man of great brightness,
And all must allow, that he shines, in politeness;
As King George hath declared to Queen Charlotte his wife,
He ne'er met with a man like Rosewarne in his life.
Then rejoice, &c. &c.

There 's Richard and Sampson and Stephen declare,
That his speeches made all the whole parliament stare;
That he knock'd down each speaker as 'twere with a
hammer,
And that all that he spoke was according to grammar.
Then rejoice, &c. &c.

They report that the Londoners say, one and all,
That we bow to Rosewarne like the wicked to Baal;
That he piles up his riches in Bodrigan-barn
That in Cornwall nought's heard but the name of
Rosewarne.
Then rejoice, &c. &c.

Folks may say that his speeches were terrible stuff -
False grammar, false English, and nonsense enough;
But if Richard tells truth I shall ne'er believe that,
As Tom Tub made them all for the poll of his hat.
Then rejoice, &c. &c.

I have heard that he hath not the soul of a cat—
In the country I grant it—but what of all that?
In the parliament (look ye) he stands like a steeple,
And roars like a bull for the good of the people.
Then rejoice, &c. &c.

And then in the church we must surely declare,
That nobody ever saw such a fine Mayor;
E'en the bagmen did never a finer cast eye on,
Where he read like a Bishop and look'd like a lion.
Then rejoice, &c. &c.

About twenty years since, both the men and the women
Swore no mortal alive could compare with old Lemon:
But now from our Magistrates gladly we learn
That old Lemon's a blockhead to Measter Rosewarne.
Then rejoice, &c. &c.

So great is his power, that, without asking for't,
He rides in his coach through the turnpikes for port;
And though 'tis a theft for which well we might try 'on,
The commissioners all are afraid to deny 'un.
Then rejoice, &c. &c.

As he knows like a King that we really regard 'un,
He declares he's asham'd of the post of vicewarden.
Is it so, Measter Morris? If that be the case,
Your servant so humble will soon have your place.
Then rejoice, &c. &c.

The best of good victuals his palace is rich in
Roast goose in the parlour, and beef in the kitchen:
Gratis all—the votes call for whatever they please;
So their hands and their chops are as busy as bees.
Then rejoice, &c. &c.

Both out-doors and in-doors, by night and by day,
The crowds and their catgut are screeching away;

Whilst the maids to each neighbour, as mute as a mouse,
Tell of measter's great feats in the parliament-house.
Then rejoice, &c. &c.

So great is his credit, he makes London town
Believe all the tin that's in Cornwall his own;
E'en a taylor that made 'un a jacket and coat
Trusted Measter Rosewarne without asking his note.
Then rejoice, &c. &c.

People say, and the tale every body believes,
That the Prince and our Measter are great as two thieves;
That Measter will give'un some pines, and get by 't
Great honours, and ride into Cornwall a Knight.
Then rejoice, &c. &c.

There's Madam will go, too, to see Measter Prince,
To show her fat sides and fine breeding and sense.
Joyce, too, will make one, and then raise her nose higher;
Good enough, after that, to be sure, for a squire.
Then rejoice, &c. &c.

Then Truro bow down to this second Colossus,
Whose greatness and cunning so deeply engross us;
Let us sing to his praise, though the county divide us—
For we must be his moyles whilst he means to bestride us.
Then rejoice, &c. &c.

 From: W. H. Thomas. *Poems of Cornwall by Thirty Cornish Authors,* 1892. A poem by M. A. Courtney.

The White Ladie.

Now, fifty years ago, may be,
On a wild winter's night,
To the ceaseless moaning of the sea,
This legend of the "White Ladie,"
Was told by firelight.

She was a proud and haughty dame
Of old Penkivell's race;
He had no son to bear his name;
He worshipped her, and who could blame,
In the old Squire's place.

Though centuries have passed away,
Her home may still be seen,
A granite building, low and grey,
Storm-beaten, often flecked with spray,
In the parish of Pendeen.

Her name was Avis; there were few
In Cornwall fair as she
Her eyes were a deep hyacinth blue,
Her cheeks had the pink creamy hue
We in the wild rose see.

Her hair was red, with gleams of gold,
And rippled round her head
But she was false,—her heart was cold;
Her soul for money she'd have sold
Pride was her daily bread.

From all the parishes around
Brave suitors came to woo
But in her sight none favour found,
She cared more for her horse and hound
Than loyal hearts and true.

Would only no denial take
Her uncle Uther's son;
He thought of her asleep, awake;
He courted dangers for her sake,
And vowed she should be won.

For her he'd often crossed the sea
In search of laces rare,

Brocades and silks, that she might be
Decked out in all her bravery,
The fairest of the fair.

For Cornishmen, in days of yore,
Thought smuggling was no crime;
And John Lenine, who knew the shore,
Had brought from France, like many more,
Rich ventures in his time.

A secret subterranean way
Ran 'twixt her house and beach;
Through a dark cave the entrance lay,
Known to few dwellers in the bay,
Most difficult to reach.

But dangers never daunted John;
By it one night he brought
Avis, when folks to rest had gone,
Some gauds she'd set her heart upon;
To win her thus he thought.

She took his gifts, but mocked his woe:
Said, "Cousin, this I'll do,
When summer comes with frost and snow,
Or roses in mid-winter blow,
Why then—I'll marry you!"

"I swear I will. Next Christmas-day
A red rose to me bring,
My answer then shall not be nay,
And as a pledge for what I say,
You may—give me a ring."

In a few days the ring was sent,
And then John sail'd afar;
In quest of the red rose he went;
To wed her still his soul was bent;

Hope was his guiding star.

He had been gone three months or more;
Christmas was drawing nigh;
Slipped in, and anchored close to shore,
A man-of-war, that once before,
In Pendeen Bay did lie.

Of her were many stories told,
How, under shade of night,
She'd sent forth men, like wolves on fold,
Who'd carried off the young and old,
For James, the King, to fight.

This dreadful ship returned again,
Made many women sad:
Some feared to lose their boys: with pain
Some wept for husbands "pressed" and slain;
Avis alone was glad.

She knew the captain, -thought that he
Could wealth and rank bestow;
For then he might her husband be,
For never wed a man would she
Who could not rent-roll show.

He was not there to woo a bride,
For men alone he came;
But still he flattered, fed her pride,
With honeyed words and gifts he plied
This most imperious dame.

Because through her he wished to learn
The secret hidden way,
From whence it ran, where made a turn,
When John was likely to return,
And why he'd gone away.

The traitress told him all—The vow

157

She'd pledged herself to keep;
Said John at home would soon be now;
Wished he would "press him", cared not how;
If killed, she should not weep.

Meanwhile poor John, who'd sailed away,
The bright, red rose to find,
Had heard in Nice a sailor say
"That roses bloomed on Christmas-day",
And Fate to him was kind.

For, walking down a crooked street,
There in a house he spied
A rose-tree bearing blossoms sweet;
He entered in with eager feet,
Nor long did there abide.

Before 'twas his, full many a crown
For that rose-bush he paid.
Quick to his ship he bore it down,
Again set sail for Penzance town,
And a prosperous voyage made.

His tree he guarded with great care,
But the flowers faded fast;
Its branches soon were nearly bare
Of all its blossoms late so fair,—
One rose remained—the last.

He reached his home on Christmas-day:
As the joy-bells out did ring;
Red rose in hand, he went his way
To meet his cousin, blithe and gay;
His heart did carols sing.

He bent his steps towards the shore
The hidden path to take,
But 'ere he reached the secret door,

Set on him ten stout men or more,
A captive him to make.

He fought for life, whilst holding still
The red rose in his hand;
And many of his foes did kill,
Was wounded oft, yet fought on, till
Lay stretched upon the sand.

He and the Captain side by side,
Both bleeding unto death.
The treachery of his would-be bride
John heard,— spake not a word, and died;
But with his dying breath.

The Captain cursed her; bade a lad
The rose to Avis bear,
Wet with his blood: "Tell her she had
Her wicked wish, might now be glad,
And it in triumph wear."

She lived till she was very old,
But never from that day
The sun shone on her; she was cold
In hottest June, for she had sold,
And sworn a life away.

No shadow from her body cast
E'er played upon the ground.
Shunned by all men, she lived alone,
And when death claimed her for his own,
Her soul no respite found.

Each Christmas morn she doth appear,
At the entrance o' the cave,
Holding her rose. She striketh fear:
Who sees her knows the coming year
Will find him in his grave.

John Trenhaile. *Dolly Pentreath and other Humorous Cornish Tales in Verse*, 1869.

But now of Doll:—to her was Christmas dear,
And rife with entertainment and good cheer
On Christmas-Eve the merry feast began,
And on to Twelfth-day jovially it ran.

One massive block of wood was placed entire
Upon her hearth, to make the festal fire.
First, on the eve it shed its heat and light,
Then blazed throughout the tide with ardour bright.

That eve would Dolly, with her kinsfolk, sit
And holy carols sing to welcome it;
While rich October, richer currant cake
Would she and all her guests, with zest partake;

And many a modern tale and legend old,
Around the fire, and o'er each cup was told;
Box, laurel, holly, decked her rooms around,
Whilst sprigs of each were to her casements bound.

On Christmas-day before the fire she placed
Her fattened goose, well peppered to her taste;
Plum pudding smoked, and luscious giblet pie,
Whose rich fragrant odours mingled in the sky

The following days from friend to friend she went,
And all in homely blessedness were spent.
Of rustic youth, a gay; theatric band,
Called "Christmas Players," walk this merry land;

Their garbs grotesque would make a cynic smile,
And their harangues the saddest heart beguile.
"Old Father Christmas," with his rude attire,
 His hideous mask, fierce mien, and club so dire,

Stalks frightful o'er the scene; while children scream.
And of the monster go to bed and dream.
St. George appears, a gay and gallant knight,
Decked out in ribbons and in linen white;

With sword of lath, and graceful in his mien,
Is heard with pleasure; with delight is seen;
He hurls defiance at each Gallic foe,
And, with his trusty sword, lays many low.

From house to house at this glad time they go,
And all these wondrous feats, and more, they show.
This entertainment much delighted Dolly,
Who, though sedate, yet loved a little folly

And who does not? with every one 'tis born
And though, too often, we have cause to mourn.
The man whom pleasantry can never charm,
 I really should approach with some alarm.

How the Parson Caught his Fish on Christmas Day - A True Story. From: *Mullyon,* by E. G. Harvey. 1869.

On Christmas morn, in sixty-nine
Not late, tho' left i' the lurch,
The Parson, he, with his Quiristers three,
Was on his way to Church.

"Look out! Look out! My Quiristers!
Look out! Look out!" quoth he,
"For the people all run to find out the fun
Whatever it may be".

"Here's Peter running down the lane -
Here's Ritchie, Sam, and John",
"Heva! Heva!" they all cry out,
Come, lev' us all be gone."

'We can't *all* go", the Parson said
"I may not go with ye,
I've others, sure, in bulk to cure,
Than the fishes o' the sea."

"We may'nt all go", the Parson said
"Ye're fishermen, and cry
Heva! Heva! when pilchards come,
But a fisher of men am I."

"Therefore, good John, while at my work,
Busy as I shall be,
While ye're afloat, and I'm at Church,
I will remember ye".

They tiled them down unto the cove
Let those rejoice that win,
For full seines three were shot i' the sea,
And the pilchards were therein.

"There's heaps o' pilchurs now", cries Tom,
"There's a passel o' pilchurs now,
There's hunderds o' hogs-heads in William's net,
And tummals under our bow".

"As putty- a sight as ever I seed",
Said John, "of a Christmas day,-
But hark to me a minute, my dears,
And mind what I do say.

The passon gain' to Church this morn,
Said he'd remember we;
So now, to kip things straight, say I,
Lev' us remember he".

And then they took of the pilchards bright
In baskets to the town,
And at the Vicarage door they laid
Their glitt'ring burden down.

"Well done! Well done! My fishers bold!"
The Parson then did say,
"Tis well you see, both for you and me
To labour and to pray".

CORNISH CHRISTMAS ABROAD

Michigan

Between the Iron and the Pine: *a biography of a pioneer family and a pioneer town*, by Lewis Charles Reimann. 1951.

"During the time that the big pine was being cut and lumbered off in the Iron River district, the iron ore lying under the entire region was discovered and exploited. Outside capital was brought in to develop mines and smelt or ship the ore. By 1900 the hills around were dotted by mine shafts, great stockpiles of red ore and even greater piles of ore rock which overlay the mineral. The shipping was done by ore trains, which hauled long strings of cars from the mines to Escanaba's giant ore docks. Here Great Lakes steamers loaded their red stuff and carried it to the steel mills which dotted the shores of this inland lake empire.

Most of the underground miners were recruited from among recent immigrants from Europe and the British Isles. "Cousin Jacks" from the copper mines of Cornwall, England, first came to the copper mines around Calumet and Houghton, then drifted to the iron mines as the copper mines became depleted or were closed by the low price of their ore. "Cousin Jacks" disdained any other work but mining. "Once a miner, always a miner" was their gospel. Italians, Austrians, Hungarians, Poles and Finns were the backbone of the labor supply. Since "Cousin Jacks" were natural miners, sober, industrious and dependable and able to converse in English, they held most of the official positions underground. They were captains, shift bosses, mechanics, "dry" superintendents, pumpmen, and "power monkeys." Religious, music lovers and nationality-conscious, they were a loyal, closed group. The "Cousin Jack" boss favored men of his own nationality and gave them preference when jobs were scarce.

"H'African Bill" was a Cousin Jack miner at the Dober mine. He kicked his H's far and wide and ate his pastie in his dinner bucket three times a week. No one ever told a taller story or had roamed a farther field than he.

Work in the underground wasn't Bill's long suit, for he had been in the British army too long, but he could sing a lusty baritone in the small Cousin Jack church choir at Christmas time. He wasn't satisfied with the vim and vigor the boys put into their choir practice.

"Why, h'over in Cornwall a man would sleep with 'is feet 'anging out of the window on cold nights for three weeks, so 'e could sing bass of Christmas Day," was Bill's choice remark."

Australia

 West Briton, 6th May 1853.

News from Australia: The following are extracts of a letter from Mr. W. H. BOASE, who emigrated from St. Ives to Australia, and dates his letter from Adelaide, January 18th, 1853. He says - "I do not regret leaving home; though I have sacrificed the comforts of Old England, I would rather be here. It is a plentiful land: there is food for the hungry and good wages for the labourer, and the master is no more independent than his servant. We arrived at Adelaide, December the 16th, after a voyage of four months, and you can imagine better than I can describe how glad we were once more to set our foot on land. The first day I went ashore I saw Capt. TREMEARNE (of St.

Ives). I went on board his vessel, and can speak well of him for his kind treatment of me; he offered to do all in his power to get me a situation". The writer then states that he went to the Burra Burra mines, where he remained about a fortnight, and was then informed that his brother had returned from the diggings, and had sent up £6 for him. On that he returned to Adelaide where he saw his brother and they were both intending the next week to go to the diggings. He found it to be a very fine country between Adelaide and the Burra Burra; sometimes over large plains as flat as a table and appearing nearly all good for cultivation. On Christmas eve they camped on an open plain, made a fire and took tea, and afterwards sang a Christmas carol, which brought into his mind many thoughts about home. It is a fine country for both shipping and farming; things at present are dear, but wages are high. Ship-carpenters' wages are from 14s. to 15s. per day; labourers in the harvest field get from 10s. to 12s. per day with rations; sawyers from 16s. to 20s. and 25s. per day.

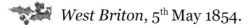 *West Briton*, 5th May 1854.

Life in Australia: The season of Christmas, just passed, would furnish us with the strongest proof of the far superior condition of the humbler classes here; and with wonder at the check to which immigration has been subjected. There were no pompous accounts of the distribution of blankets, for there are no poor to be humiliated by the receptions of alms. No long narration of parish banquets, with their measured ounces of meat, swelled out columns, for most fortunately we have no necessity for such an institution. No miserable outcasts, shivering in a bleak winter's wind, made us almost ashamed of the comforts of our own home. On every side there were happy radiant faces, and we feel sure that there was not one person in health in the whole colony who could not on that day afford a hearty dinner to his family.

In confirmation of our statements we need only direct the attention of our English readers to the table of wages published in another column. Carpenters are earning from GBP7 to GBP9 per week, masons from nine to ten guineas, blacksmiths from GBP6 to GBP7. 10s., many of the compositors in our office earn from GBP10 to GBP12 a week. In the single item of the pay given to labourers on the public roads, since our last summary we find an increase of from 8s. a day to 12s. and 15s.; and we feel confident that there is not a labouring man in this colony who cannot, by industry and economy, at the end of the year, put by from his earnings a sum in pounds which in England the same man might count himself happy to have saved in pence.

 West Briton, 2nd June 1854.

Incidents of Colonial Life: A young gentleman of Geelong, Australia, writing to a relative at home, under date of January, 1856, says:- I had invitations from different persons to spend my Christmas at their stations in the bush. But I had had sufficient experience of that kind of thing to know, that three or four days of Christmas spent with a settler would settle me for a fortnight, and I therefore stopped at home, and this is the way my Christmas went. My Irish neighbours (with whom he boards while lodging in weather boarded rooms of his own) considered it better to keep up Christmas eve than Christmas day, and the young widow aforesaid, her sister, and four others came up to dance, sing, eat cake and drink strong punch. We commenced at ten, and, so far as I was concerned, left off at three next morning, when I went to bed. Getting up at eight, I found my young widow busy stuffing a goose, and the others culinarily employed, and, much to my surprise, I learnt that none of them had been to bed. For, intending to go to mass on Christmas day, after the manner, I suppose, of the Irish, they had been afraid to go to bed lest they should miss it - mass commencing at five in the morning - and had kept themselves dancing and romping all through the night. Well, I breakfasted, and in order the better to enjoy my dinner, I took a long walk, returning about two, thinking we were to have a downright Christmas dinner. Christmas eve, however, had been too much for my neighbours. They were all sound asleep, except the little ones, and the consequence was that I sat down alone before a huge goose, a boiled turkey, a large ham, and a vast plum pudding. At public dinners there is usually a band in attendance; on the present occasion the music that I had was such as is caused by the loud breathing of persons asleep. That was my first specimen of an Irish Christmas; and remarkably Irish I consider it to be.